THE ORCHARD ALMANAC

A Spraysaver Guide

Published by Spraysaver Publications
Rockport, Maine 04856

Distributed by Spraysaver Publications
Erle, Québec J0B3J0

Dépôt legal — 2e trimestre 1986
Bibliotèque nationale du Québec

Legal deposit — 2nd quarter 1986
National Library of Canada

Library of Congress Catalog Card Number 86-60398

ISBN 0-9616523-0-6

This book is dedicated to pioneers in ecological orchard management who have inspired us:

Peter Escher, Alvin Filsinger, A.D. Pickett,

A.P. Thompson, and Stuart Hill.

Table of Contents

Acknowledgements

We would like to thank Susan Boyer who designed this book, Cynthia Anthony and Janet Motyer who proofread the numerous revisions, Polly Warren who created the illustrations, and Paula Whittet who processed the manuscript.

We would like to acknowledge Dr. Stuart Hill, Bart Hall-Beyer, Alice Bennett-Groh, Hugh Williams, George Scalf, and Dr. Frank Eggert for reviewing the rough draft. The authors, however, remain solely responsible for the text and will attribute technical inaccuracies and poetic excesses to each other.

Other people who have helped us over the years are Chaitanya York, Tony Bok, Dr. W.E. MacLellan, Dr. Ken Sanford, Grace Gershuny, Renee Vickery, John Harker and Michael Schuster.

About the Authors

Stephen Page is an environmental designer and landscape contractor based in Rockport on the coast of Maine. He planted his first orchard in 1974, another in 1976, and has leased other orchards in addition to contracting his orchard management services. In the winter he writes articles on various horticultural subjects for several magazines. Active in the Maine Organic Farmers and Gardeners Association, Steve is currently working for farmland preservation and land stewardship trusts.

Joseph Smillie has been a consultant in ecological agriculture since 1977, specializing in soil fertility, composting systems, biological apple management, foliar fertilization, and organic certification. He is currently the chairperson of the Certification Review Committee for the Organic Food Production Association of North America. Joe tends his orchard and homesteads with his family on a plateau in Erle, Quebec.

Joseph Smillie and Stephen Page

Foreword

Progress toward more responsible behavior can always be traced to courageous actions of individuals - often carried out in the face of what can seem like insurmountable odds against their being successful. I have known the courageous authors of this book for over ten years and have followed their separate and combined struggles to make our world a better and safer place - in this case through the development of a more rational approach to pest control in orchards, involving particularly a reduction in our dependence on toxic chemical solutions. I would like to add a few words of my own to theirs in the hope that it will make this goal more achievable.

Today, pests are usually seen as enemies and pest control as the use of science and technology to repress them. While great successes have been achieved by following this approach, there have also been numerous problems including damage to human health, to non-target species including beneficial organisms and the development of additional pest problems. Recognition of this situation has led to the development of integrated pest management (IPM), an approach designed to retain the benefits of the previous methods of control and to minimize the problems. Although progress has been made in this direction there remain inherent problems, particularly because of the continued dependence of IPM on curative solutions. The alternative approach, which I advocate, is to develop preventative solutions. Whereas curative approaches tend to be generated within disciplines, preventative solutions are transdisciplinary and involve the redesign of whole systems.

The way we view pests in many ways determines how we control them. By viewing them as enemies we are likely to be attracted to quick, curative, imported solutions based on single, simple, direct, high power actions involving physics or chemistry and high technology. Such actions are taken in the context of an aggressor-victim relationship with the pest. We are fighting a war in which we get the pest or it gets us.

Contrast this with the situation in which the grower has a philosophy that the earth is his or her home in which all the organisms, in one way or another, are allies, i.e., there are no enemies. In this case the pests would be viewed as an indicator that a correction needs to be made in the design and/or management of the orchard. While short term actions to control the pests may be taken, these would be selected to avoid damaging the integrity of the whole system and the primary ongoing effort will be focused on responding to the causes of the problem. This will tend to foster the pursuit of long term solutions based on multi-faceted, indirect, low power actions involving biology, ecology, knowledge, skills and local resources. The test, for me, of the difference between preventative and curative approaches is that the former, because of its reliance on long term, indirect solutions tends to be conducted "anonymously," i.e., there is no obvious, simple connection between the actions of the grower and the reduction of the pest. Rather, by restoring and supporting the natural balance within the system, the pest population, no longer needing to indicate an imbalance, declines. The grower is rather like the great leader spoken of in early eastern writing, in which it was said, "of a great leader, the people will say we did it ourselves" or, to reword it for our situation, "of a great grower, the orchard will appear to solve its own problems." Contrast this with the "magic bullet" pesticide solution that is far from anonymous.

Another important difference is that whereas the pesticide solution must be repeated and constantly revised as the pest inevitably becomes resistant, the preventative solution is usually permanent and need only be refined.

When looking for causes of pest outbreaks we need to consider such aspects as plant selection, site selection and preparation, planting design and site maintenance including especially soil conditions, pruning, groundcover management, removal of fallen fruit, the introduction of biological control agents for important pests, and winter protection of trees.

The aim of such an approach is to design systems that are capable of solving their pest problems "internally" as opposed to relying on direct intervention from the outside. Thus the system would be designed to contain sufficient feedback loops in the form of natural controls such that if a potential pest population began to increase, it would soon be repressed because of the constant availability of the natural control. Furthermore the crop would be less attractive to pests, less stressed and less susceptible to significant damage. Such an approach places humans within rather than outside the system being managed. In this position we are likely to witness the mutually supportive co-evolution of person and planet.

It is possible that the above ideas may bring up feelings of hope and/or cynicism. I like to think that hope comes from my true being that sees reality as it actually is, and that cynicism is merely the residue of past experiences in which those who influenced my development failed to recognize that both people and the planet are benign.

The words of the psychologist R.D. Laing are perhaps helpful in solving this riddle. He suggests that during our development it is as if each of us were hypnotized twice: firstly into accepting pseudoreality as reality, and secondly into believing that we were not hypnotized. With these thoughts I commend this book to you and encourage you to deepen the intimacy of your relationship with your orchard and its inhabitants, even the pests.

Dr. Stuart B. Hill
Associate Professor of Entomology
Director of Ecological Agriculture Projects
Macdonald College of McGill University
St. Anne de Bellevue, Quebec Canada
3 April 1986

Introduction

The life of the orchard is revealed to those who take the time to amble open minded down the rows of trees. Nature's patterns are incredibly complex and interwoven, a tapestry too fine to be fully comprehended. Yet there is a pattern, and as surely as bud turns to bloom we can learn to recognize the fibers in the weave. Competing for the abundant energy of the trees and the fruit are many varmints, insects, mites and other organisms that work against the orchardist's desire to grow fruit for the cold cellar. The inhabitants of the orchard are not difficult to recognize. Their distinctive signatures weave a pattern on the loom of the tree, tying together limbs, buds, leaves and fruit. How we react to these "pests" reflects the values we put on the art of growing with, not against, the designs of nature.

Since World War II many synthetic pesticides (including insecticides, fungicides, herbicides, acaricides and nematicides) have been used in orchards in an attempt to eradicate pests. This approach has proven costly, dangerous and unsuccessful. The term "pest" is an economic and not a biological description, but pesticides cannot discriminate in this way. The increased use of pesticides has not reduced the level of pest damage but created the need for more and stronger pesticides because of the destruction of the natural enemy complex and increased pest resistance. This "pesticide treadmill," as entomologist Robert Van den Bosch has noted, only benefits the pesticide companies while damaging the ecosystem.

In order to change the vicious cycle of increased chemical use, orchardists need to make a transition to more environmentally sound methods. The first practical step is the adoption of Integrated Pest Management (I.P.M.) techniques. The decreased spray costs and lower residue levels make this transition not only ecological but profitable. It has become increasingly obvious that the future of pest management does not lie with the short term solution of more powerful pesticides but with long term understanding of the insects, mites, fungi and other organisms that share the orchard.

This almanac offers an I.P.M. approach of reduced chemical sprays or an "organic" method of natural controls. The word "organic" is used because of its general public acceptance. The terms "ecological," "biological," and "regenerative," or "sustainable" can often be interchanged with more accuracy. Ecological orchard management depends on designing a self-regulating system of natural controls which rely on prevention rather than eradication. At present organic orchardists lack effective control procedures for some insects and diseases. Market demand for residue-free fruit will fund the development of these systems. An ecological approach not only requires a knowledge of insect and disease cycles, an understanding of spray materials and skill in marketing, but a strong commitment to a wholistic way of thinking.

There is a big orchard lying dormant now. It is the orchard of millions of over-sprayed or under-cared-for trees that can be coaxed back to a natural balance and fruitfulness with a gentle hand, some record keeping and a desire to learn to see. In a few years of following the rhythm of the orchard season it is possible to learn the patterns of the pest and beneficial forms of orchard life. By entering into a close relationship with some of the threads that create the natural pattern, the aware orchardist becomes more than a technician of poisons. One enters the weave personally. The enemy is no longer the pests but our own ignorance and inability to clearly see the beauty of the whole cloth.

There will always be a need to manage the pests and diseases that harm the fruit trees and the crops which we have worked hard to grow. Learn to use a light touch with pest management, a direct and meaningful intervention rather than the blind broad strokes of weekly poison sprays. The reward for your discretion will be a harvest of knowledge and health, and a heritage of fertile soils to give to our children.

How To Use This Almanac

We call this book an almanac because it follows the seasons. It is cyclical in nature and has no real beginning or ending. In the various essays some concepts are repeated. We have cross-referenced related topics so that you can refer to the section with the greatest detail. For example, pesticides are mentioned throughout the text but the month of November contains the bulk of the information on pesticides. Although the authors have tried to modify their regional bias toward apple trees, it has shown throughout the work on this book.

The goal of this almanac is simply to give you information on what to do when. Since timing is critical in orchard management, and since most of the dates given are for central New England, you must adjust accordingly, and look ahead a few weeks if need be. The most critical timing is around bud development and bloom — you have to look at your own trees to know your schedule. Use the average dates of bloom, the degree day figures and other information for approximations of timing. With experience you will have a good schedule on which to base your management program.

You will find that keeping records is indispensible. As the season progresses record the timing of the bud stages, the temperature, the time of bloom, the weather, the times that you spray, what you spray, and the insect cycles. Note the timing of fertilizer applications. Keep a record of when different varieties ripen and when they are harvested. Your orchard deserves this record, and you will find it an extremely useful management tool in future years.

Keeping track of degree days will take much of the guesswork out of predicting your spray schedule. One can safely predict that bloom will occur when 430 degree days above 40 degrees F. have accumulated. Plum curculio will emerge when 300 degree days have accumulated and control of this pest should begin when the 320 degree day mark is reached. The dates will vary every year, but the plants and the insects are predictable in their response to the season's ambient temperature. Using this information and your observations in the field, you will be well on your way to developing your own schedule.

Many state and provincial pomologists provide a call-in phone line for growers that supplies the latest information on pest emergence. The information is usually updated once or twice a week so that growers can keep abreast of developments in the area. It is helpful to use the services of a more southerly zone to anticipate your conditions before they happen. Call your local extension pomologist to get information on what is available in your area. Neighbors and local orchardists are a valuable source of information and advice. Often their sense of timing is more accurate for your area than state or provincial dates, especially where there is a wide range of climates.

This book is part of what you need to manage your orchard ecologically. The development of your powers of observation is essential. Walking through the orchard on a regular basis, you will become sensitive to the subtle changes that signal new stages of development. By looking closely at the twigs, the foliage and the fruit, you will learn to recognize symptoms of problems before they become irreversible. Soon you will develop an awareness of the whole tree environment, and you will be able to see with a new sharpness of the senses.

JANUARY

- Organic Controls or Pesticides — The Choices
- The Nova Scotia Experience
- Pruning Tips
- Sanitation

Wassail, the ancient practice of beating the limbs of fruit trees with wooden sticks, was a twelfth-night ritual said to waken the trees to the new year. Fill the bowls with ale, and give the trees Wassail.				1	2	3
4	5	6	7	8	9	10
Cut and burn dead fruitwood.						
11	12	13	14	15	16	17
		Read a book about pruning.				
18	19	20	21	22	23	24
Order nursery stock early.			Pack snow around trunks, check for mice, deer, and rabbits.			
25	26	27	28	29	30	31
Hold off pruning for now. Read another book.				Collect scions for grafting.		

January

Skiing through the orchard at this time of year can be exhilarating when the snow is deep and fresh. I marvel at the life lying dormant in the winter orchard. I worry about the not-so-dormant life too. Underneath the snow cover mice are foraging for food, and I'm glad for the wire mesh which protects the tender bark of the new trees. I see in one corner of the orchard that deer have gotten through the fence where a drift has buried two wires and the top wire, though charged, wasn't enough to stop them. Time to add yet another wire to defense.

Cozy within the litter in the woods surrounding the orchard plum curculio are overwintering. I suspect that they have gathered under the leaf litter beneath the tall maple on the edge of the woodlot. Now that the trees have hardened off well, I hope for some really cold weather. Here in the north a good cold winter can wipe out many curculios. Earlier, I heard a woodpecker on one of the older trees, probably looking for codling moth cocoons under the scales of bark or drilling for borers. I'll keep some suet in woody's feeder to whet his appetite and keep him around.

In the frozen ground, somehow surviving the freezing and thawing, are the ubiquitous apple maggot pupae, some of which will go through two winters in the soil before hatching into the adult flies. That is a long rest, which probably explains their survivability. On the branches of the tree itself are egg masses, and a careful scan with my hand lens reveals some aphid eggs on the leaders of the young trees, a few tent caterpillar egg masses, and one tree has quite a few mite eggs which turn the terminal branches rusty. I tie an orange ribbon on this tree to mark it for dormant oil spray in the spring.

Spring is a long way off still, and I'm glad because I have a lot to do to prepare for the season ahead. The orchard may be dormant now, but the days are getting longer and dormant problems are going to be live ones soon enough.

Terminal growth of an apple twig showing fruiting spurs.

Organic Controls or Pesticides — The Choices

There is no easy way to grow high quality fruit — there are too many pests and diseases that want to get at the fruit first. For the past fifty years the answer to the pest problem has been to spray orchards with a wide variety of chemicals in order to eliminate most or all insects and diseases. Massive doses of lead arsenate, then DDT and now Guthion, together with weekly doses of fungicides created very fragile monocultures and new problems developed.

Integrated Pest Management (IPM) was the response to the problem. According to the *I.P.M. Practitioner,* "Integrated Pest Management is a process for deciding IF pest supression treatments are needed, WHEN they should be initiated, WHERE they should be applied, and WHAT strategy and mix of tactics to use." In IPM programs, natural controls are combined with a minimal amount of pesticides and only those pesticides are used which have a low "eco-profile" and do not injure beneficial species. IPM is only effective where insect populations are carefully monitored and economic thresholds have been established.

Until recently the grower who has chosen not to use chemicals hasn't had much choice as far as management technique that enables him to get a marketable crop. This book outlines a management program that under most circumstances will result in a certifiably organic crop. The products and practices that are eligible for organic production systems vary slightly depending on the certifying organization, regional association, or government regulation. It is the responsibility of these organizations to make decisions in controversial areas. For example, the definition of processed or synthetic fertilizers has many "grey areas." Synthetic pesticides are not acceptable in any certified organic program. The certification process accents the positive methods a grower uses in the production of high-quality, residue-free fruit.

Most IPM programs rely upon some synthetic pesticides, although they are used in reduced volumes. Choosing the pesticide route, even with IPM practices, means that the grower needs to study carefully the proper methods of handling, diluting, applying and disposing of pesticides. It means that the grower must monitor the effects of his sprays on beneficial organisms so as to disrupt as little as possible the natural balances in the orchard. Finally, it means that the grower must accept that he is using a short-term solution to the problem, and that if the chemical program is discontinued the problems will get much worse before natural balances are restored.

In this book there are two approaches for every problem. Those choosing to use the certifiably organic program must follow it closely to get good results. Others may choose to use chemicals for some problems, developing their own IPM program to meet their needs. In any case, organic or chemical, orchardists must carefully learn to know their own trees and the natural organisms that live on those trees. No matter what you spray, you must spray regularly, with appropriate timing, to maintain your orchard properly.

The Nova Scotia Experience

The Annapolis Valley of Nova Scotia was at one time the most concentrated fruit growing area in Canada. Before 1900 very little spraying for pest control was done. Records show that serious damage to fruit and foliage often occurred. Pesticide use became intensive by the 1940 s, at the same time as in the U.S., but a problem developed — the codling moth damage increased from insignificant proportions to one-third of the total crop in 1948, despite increased dosages of DDT. Now we know that DDT was partially the cause of this increase because it eliminated natural predators of the moth.

Growers and scientists in Nova Scotia developed a pest control program unique in North America after World War II. This was the first example of a completely integrated pest management system. The entomologists established this program based on natural controls before chemical company salesmen took over. In other parts of the world chemical salesmen were aggressively molding growers' opinions. There were few who spoke for natural controls.

A.D. Pickett, W.E. MacLellan, and others from the Research Station in Kentville, Nova Scotia, began in 1943 to study the populations of 73 species of insects and mites which were prevalent on apples. The weakness of chemical controls of pests became apparent, especially the detrimental effects of chemicals on beneficial organisms.

The researchers looked at the total orchard ecosystem, finding 98 different species of arthropods on a single unsprayed tree. This ecosystem was a balance of pests, predators, and parasites. The balance was always changing, but remained within certain parameters. Broad spectrum chemicals always left an imbalance, destroying the natural controls as well as the intended pests. When selective insecticides were used instead of broad spectrum chemicals, pests were kept at a reasonable economical level by natural predators.

During changeovers to natural/chemical integrated spray programs some specific isolated outbreaks of pests occurred. These were controlled by broad spectrum pesticides. Although just one application of a broad spectrum insecticide would cause some damage to beneficial organisms, the integrated orchards responded with a remarkable resilience. Natural predators quickly returned to balance the pests. Natural controls worked best, and when aided with an extremely light hand with the sprayer growers could make money.

A substantial switch was made to the integrated control program in 1954, the first year that ryania was used to control codling moth. After the switch, the number of bees visiting apple blossoms in the valley increased five fold. Today almost half the acreage is monitored, and on this acreage commercial apple growers average less than three insecticide applications.

Between 1954 and today there has been a lot of hard work by entomologists and pathologists who seek alternatives to chemical pesticides. Every state and province has more individuals every year working toward economical, natural pest control. Growers are learning to monitor insects and disease so that they can decide when to spray. Commercial fruit growers are substantially cutting the amounts of poison in their orchards. Integrated Pest Management has become economically attractive as well as ecologically sound.

Pruning Tips

Rather than write about our personal approach to pruning, we recommend spending a winter reading about pruning and looking at the trees. You might know of an orchardist who would let you watch him prune. There are many teachers and we are still learning. Libraries are full of pruning books. *Ecological Fruit Production in the North* has an excellent study by Jean Richard. Hilltop Nurseries in Hartford, Michigan, has a detailed young tree training program in their catalog. You should learn what is best for your trees.

Healthy fruit trees tend to grow more vegetative growth than fruit if left untended. With a life span of many decades, the tree's biological imperative is to grow large in its youth, then seed and reproduce later.

Pruning is the art of removing unwanted tree structure, and the conscientious grower will discover that the art is rewarding. Every tree is a unique sculpture and once the growing process is understood growth can be directed for the health of the tree and the pruner.

● It is better to remove a whole branch than to leave a stub.

● Leave a clean cut from which water will drain.

● Don't prune fruit trees in the fall or early winter. Chances of winterkill are drastically increased by fall pruning.

● Never prune off more than a third of new growth on a branch or a third of the new wood in a tree. For beginners, a quarter would be more appropriate.

● Prune branches that rub against each other or those so close together that one completely shades the other.

● A branch with a vertical fork is likely to split if loaded with fruit or ice. Select one or the other to keep, favoring the lower branch if the object is to keep the tree's height down.

● Some people use pruning paint, some don't. There are more opinions as to its efficacy than varieties of apples. On my young trees, when a cut is exposed to the sun I use white interior latex to cover the wound. The white reflects sunlight which otherwise can split the bark.

● Cherry trees need little pruning after the first five years. Limit pruning to removal of dead wood, excess growth, and interfering branches. Allow sunlight into the tree.

● Pear trees should be pruned lightly. The growth habit of pears is upright, with naturally narrow crotches. Thin out the top of the tree to allow light in, and remove all suckers and dead wood. If fire blight is a problem, pruning tools must be sterilized in alcohol or 1:10 bleach solution between making the next cut.

● Plum trees bear fruit on spurs, usually in the interior of the tree. If these spurs have become unfruitful they should be removed, favoring the healthy, bearing spurs. If an old plum tree is bearing many small inferior fruit, remove one third of the spurs. Nip back one-fourth to one third of the new growth to encourage spur production.

● Peach trees need more pruning than other fruits. They also have a much shorter life expectancy, and little can be done to restore an old peach tree so that it bears well. All fruit of the peach tree is borne on new (last season's) wood. Always favor new wood, removing older branches which will not bear again. Thin where necessary to allow maximum penetration of the sun; favor new, vigorous branches rising from the trunk; nip back one third of all new growth. Peach wood is more brittle than other fruitwood, and peaches tend to overbear, so thinning the fruit is especially important to prevent branches from breaking. Thinning also prevents the possibility of winter damage from depleted carbohydrate reserves.

● Observe where the flower buds are formed on the tree, noting where and on what age wood these buds are found. Attempt to distribute the flower buds and new shoot growth evenly throughout the tree, making sure each bud is as open to the sunlight as possible. This can be accomplished by proper pruning and training of the tree, with renewal of fruiting branches from time to time.

Sanitation

Sanitation will be mentioned often throughout the almanac. This practice is the basis for all reduced-pesticide management programs. Sanitation refers to the practice of: 1) knowing when disease spores or insect larvae are present and vulnerable; 2) cleaning them up; and 3) disposing of them. This almanac will help you learn the pest cycles.

Disposal of disease or insect infested tree parts is an individual matter, often depending on the scale of the orchard. Chris Granstrom has told of old-timers who wheeled portable incinerators through the orchards to burn prunings. Burning is always a good option, even if a parlor woodstove is where the burning takes place. Leaves can be burned as well as woody stems and branches.

Feeding disposable fruit to animals is a good way to eliminate insect larvae and fungus. Be cautious introducing a new element to your animal's rations. My cow was never cautious, and would usually overdose on fruit and pomace if given a chance. Pigs will characteristically gorge and then lose interest.

Taking orchard waste to the dump is another option, but my town's landfill is too near and I know that the pests will return to another orchard, if not mine. Some dumps have incinerators, which is a good solution. If you are disposing of wormy fruit, seal it in plastic bags to kill the insect larvae. I've found that the larvae-ridden fruit ferment in plastic bags, pickling the worms inside. After a year, I turn the pulp into the compost or mulch the blueberries with it.

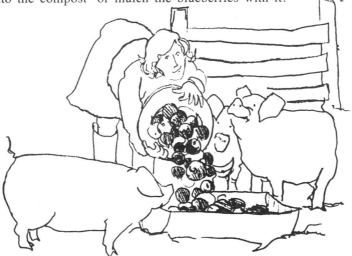

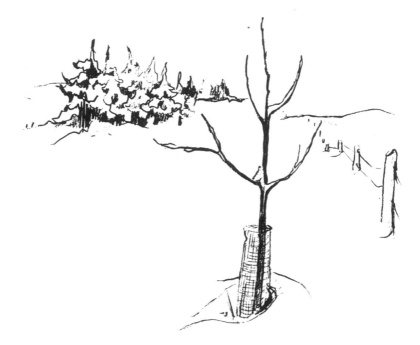

FEBRUARY

- New Trees — Fungicide Free Orchards

- Orchard Soil Fertility

- Restoring Old Trees

- Dormant Season Insect Control

- Degree Days

				1	2	3
				Pack snow around trunks below mouse guards.		
4	5	6	7	8	9	10
Write up a proposed pest and fertilizer spray program.						
11	12	13	14	15	16	17
	Begin pruning all fruits except peaches.			Purchase pesticides early, ask for fresh stock.		
18	19	20	21	22	23	24
"Mummified" fruit in trees are sources of fungus. Dispose of in sealed plastic bags.					Collect scions.	
25	26	27	28			
Severe pruning means you must use less nitrogen.						

February

I plant new trees every year, to replace older trees that I am culling out and to experiment with new varieties. If I am trying a new rootstock, or buying many trees of one variety, I order two years in advance to get the grafting done by a good custom nursery. I love to graft trees, but I know that the professionals do it more consistently. The good nurseries deliver strong trees ready to grow. Still, I will take a few scions this month to store in the refrigerator and to pass on to friends.

I discourage people from buying fruit trees at garden centers. I've watched as employees at one of these "fast food" nurseries ruthlessly hacked bare root stock to get it to fit into a tiny fibre pot, then filled the pot with sand and peat. They didn't prune back the top at all (the bigger the better for sales) and then the tree was set aside in the row to be alternately dried out and soaked. I don't wonder that many people have been discouraged trying to grow fruit trees which they bought unknowingly.

Mail order nurseries usually ship quality bare root stock, which has a much better chance of thriving if it is planted quickly, directly in the permanent location. No matter how good the stock is I regard mail order plants as traumatized patients needing immediate intensive care. Considering that the trees were machine dug in autumn, stored in refrigeration all winter, and finally subjected to the vagaries of the post office or UPS, it is a wonder that they pull through at all. The miracle is that they thrive if properly planted and cared for.

My fruit trees hardened off well last December, and have stayed consistently cold since, so I may start pruning later this month. As I walk past the young trees I planted last year I shape them up with my eyes but spare the knife. I will start pruning the older ones first, saving the tender young ones for March and April. There is no need to hurry pruning, and I'm still busy keeping rodents away. I fuss a lot over the young trees, because I've found that without exception the trees that had the best start are the ones that give the best harvest in later years.

New Trees — Fungicide Free Orchards

John Harker at Highmoor Farm has suggested: "A responsible home orchardist will plant three types of trees: 1) the disease resistant varieties, such as those offered by New York State Fruit Testing Association, 2) local wild selections of particular merit, 3) old varieties that are time-proven and adapted." Planting new trees is a continuous process — I start in the fall, preparing the holes for spring planting. See August for "Special Care for Young Trees," and September for "Planting Preparation."

A major advancement in fruit science has been the breeding program which has developed new varieties, genetically resistant to diseases. Since 1970 growers have been able to plant apple varieties that need no expensive and time consuming fungicide sprays. The savings from the elimination of fungicides is not only economic — without fungicides beneficial soil organisms can play their important role in maintaining a natural, balanced ecosystem.

Although modern monitoring and forecasting techniques (including climate interpretation and scab spore level measurements) can reduce the amount of fungicide needed to combat diseases, new varieties are the real hope for future fungicide-free orchards. Most standard varieties will always need fungicides, except in isolated locations where scab spore levels are minimal. Until resistant varieties were developed (almost twenty years ago) it seemed that fungicides would forever be a part of orchard management.

The first program to begin breeding disease resistance in apples began in 1945 with three experimental stations cooperating: Purdue, Illinois, and New Jersey. Since then many other states and Canadian provinces have joined in the effort. Thousands of trees have been started from seed in an effort to breed a commercially acceptable market apple from the inedible crabapples which first showed signs of disease resistance.

Breeding resistance to disease has some problems. The time involved in breeding new varieties of fruit trees is considerable. It can be six to eight years from seed to fruit as opposed to the annual or biennial fruiting of most vegetable crops. This time lag is probably the greatest hindrance in breeding programs. It took 25 years to develop Prima, which became available in 1970 as the first commercial quality disease resistant apple variety.

The total bill for developing the Prima apple variety came to more than two million dollars. Once the groundwork was done, however, new disease resistant varieties have been appearing quickly. Many nurseries are now offering several disease resistant varieties in their catalogs. Dozens of other resistant varieties are available from organizations such as the New York Fruit Testing Cooperative Association (Geneva N.Y. 14456).

Commercial orchardists are reluctant to plant new varieties because they foresee marketing problems. The American consumer is very hesitant to buy an unknown variety of apple. Small orchardists and homesteaders, on the other hand, are learning that they can save a lot of time and money by planting varieties that don't need to be sprayed for disease. I have found no problem marketing my Prima apples, and I'm even more enthusiastic about the Liberty fruit, which I harvested for the first time last year. Rumor has it that Freedom is even better. No fungicides, no scab, and delicious fruit. That's progress.

Disease Resistant Varieties

Fruit/ Disease	Resistant Varieties	Susceptible Varieties
APPLE:		
Scab	Liberty*, Prima*, Priscilla*, MacFree*, Nova Easygro*, Freedom*, Grimes Golden*, York Imperial*, Ingraham*, Jonathan, Golden Delicious, Wagener, Yellow Transparent, Astrachan, Gravenstein, Wealthy, Baldwin	MacIntosh, Delicious, Rome, Winesap, Northern Spy, Cortland, Macoun, Mutsu, Idared, Empire, Jerseymac
Fire blight	Liberty*, MacFree*, Prima*, Priscilla*, Nova Easygro, Winesap, NW Greening, Delicious, Grimes Golden, Northern Spy, Empire, Stayman, Baldwin, Duchess, Ben Davis	Granny Smith, Rome, Golden Delicious, York, Wealthy, Mutsu, Lodi, Beacon, Jonathan, Yellow Transparent, Idared, R.I. Greening, Twenty Ounce, Tompkins King
Cedar rust	Liberty*, Priscilla*, Nova, Easygro*, Baldwin, MacIntosh, Delicious	Prima, Golden Delicious
Powdery mildew	Liberty*, Prima*, Sir Prize*, Golden Delicious, Spartan, Delicious, Lodi	Cortland, Rome, MacIntosh, Jonathan, Baldwin, Idared, Monroe
PEAR:		
Fire blight	Moonglow, Devoe, Maxine, Gorham, Magness, Kieffer, Seckel, Tyson, Old Home, Orient, Ure, Golden Spice	Bartlett, Bosc, Anjou, Clapps Favorite, Flemish Beauty
PLUM:		
Black knot	Shiro*, Santa Rosa*, Formosa*, President*, Methley, Milton, Early Italian, Bradshaw, Fellenberg	Stanley, Blufre, Shropshire, Damson
PEACH:		
Powdery mildew		Redskin, Reo-Oso-Gem

*Indicates high resistance or immunity.
Many new varieties not on this list are being tested.
Note that resistance to disease varies from place to place and according to the amount of disease inoculum present. Also, different strains of the various cultivars show varying degrees of resistance. Do not put all your eggs in one basket: try several varieties and see which works best for you.
Feedback from readers regarding experiences with new and old varieties would be appreciated.

Orchard Soil Fertility

Fertilization begins before the orchard is planted and continues yearly thereafter. This involves a great deal more effort than simply putting some mineral fertilizer in the planting hole. The basis of biological fruit production (including insect control) rests on the premise that a healthy tree grows from a healthy soil and is more resistant to insects and diseases.

A fertile soil teems with life, from bacteria to earthworms, that feed on organic matter and mineral nutrients and create a vital humus. Orchard site preparation should be started one or two growing seasons before the trees are planted by turning the sod, and tilling in various green manure crops along with animal manures and mineral amendments.

A soil test, either from extension services, university or private laboratories, will help determine which minerals need to be added. If the pH is below 6.5 limestone should be added in amounts that will "sweeten" the soil to above 6.5. Limestone not only neutralizes acid soil but also adds essential calcium. If the soil test shows low levels of magnesium then dolomitic limestone (which contains magnesium and calcium) should be used.

Optimum fruit production depends on proper balance of the three major cations (positively-charged elements) calcium, magnesium and potassium. Sulfate of potash-magnesia (brand names Sul-po-mag and K-Mag) is an effective orchard fertilizer for soils low in magnesium and potassium.

A soil pH that is over 7 makes it difficult for the tree roots to absorb trace elements. Alkaline soil will probably also have an excess of calcium and magnesium greatly reducing the availability of potassium. In this case it may be necessary to foliar feed trace elements and add appropriate amounts of potassium sulfate. In the unlikely case that calcium is low then agricultural gypsum (calcium sulfate) should be applied.

Conventional blends of N-P-K fertilizers like 10-10-10 are not suited to orchards. The nitrogen is often in a form unsuitable for fruit trees, the phosphorus is not necessary in most cases and the potassium is usually in a chloride form which is the least favorable for fruit production.

Nitrogen can be supplied to the orchard by the incorporation of green and animal manures in the preparation phase and, on a regular basis, by compost mulches. A fertile soil will release nitrogen to the tree at a steady rate throughout the season. If nitrogen needs to be supplemented it can be done with fertilizers such as calcium nitrate, potassium nitrate or ammonium sulfate depending on soil pH and other mineral needs. Foliar sprays of urea or fish emulsion can also be applied if necessary. Excessive nitrogen can be a problem negatively affecting winter hardiness, fruit storage and insect and fire blight resistance. Use nitrogen fertilizers carefully addressing known needs rather than blanket applications. Healthy trees will often run a little on the lean side with respect to nitrogen.

Phosphorus is best supplied by applications of rock phosphate (in low pH soils) during the green manure preparation phase. Mature apple trees rarely show any need for supplemental phosphorus. The available phosphorus necessary for root development in young whips can be supplied by bone meal mixed in with the roots at planting.

Specific micro-nutrient needs can be supplied by granular fertilizers or foliar sprays. A thick compost mulch spread in a four foot circle around new trees will supply nutrients and greatly increase the biological activity in the fruit trees' root zone.

Annual leaf analysis is the best way of monitoring the tree's mineral needs. By analyzing the leaf tissue a laboratory can determine what the tree roots are able to garner from the soil reserves regardless of what the soil test says is available. After years of research standards for ideal mineral levels have been established for many fruits. Leaf testing services of state or provincial governments provide sampling instructions. The combination of a soil test and leaf analysis along with careful observation by the orchardist provides a firm basis for mineral supplementation.

Restoring Old Trees

Many people think about pruning when they look at a neglected old tree. I like to delay pruning live wood until I'm sure that the tree I'm restoring is in good health. Too often I've seen a heavy pruning followed by years of nonproductive growth as the tree adjusts to the stimulus of pruning. A healthy vigorous tree can be pruned without harm, but a weak tree should be brought back to health before feeling the saw. Until a declining tree starts putting out healthy new foliage it needs all the leaf area that is present. Turn your attention to the soil first.

The roots of old fruit trees are at least as extensive as the branches, with some important differences. About 80 percent of the feeding roots lie within the top eight inches of soil around the drip-line circumference of the tree. Deeper roots anchor the tree and supply it with water. An often overlooked reason for poor production in older trees is that this mass of roots has depleted the nutrients available in the soil. Compost, a good hay mulch and foliar feeding program are the first requirements of an aging fruit tree.

Production should not be the only goal when working on old trees. If production is all you want, you will be much better off planting young trees and waiting a few years. The value of old trees is in their beauty, in the preservation of old varieties and in the satisfaction of gathering a humble harvest of good quality.

Restoring old fruit trees requires considerable effort, so the first question is whether the old tree is worth keeping at all. Ask yourself: Is the tree actively growing or is it in a state of decline? Is it an asset to the landscape? Beauty is more subjective than health. I tend to be critical of shape. Some trees have no pleasing shape and are just plain ugly. Unless such a tree is bearing a wonderful crop, I see no reason not to give it a tree's final glory — in the fireplace on Christmas Eve. Plant a new tree and train it well.

One way I judge a tree's health is by measuring the length of the current season's branch growth. On apples, I like to see twelve to sixteen inches from the annual growth ring to the terminal bud at the end of a season. Less than four inches of new growth tells me that the tree is losing ground.

There are many reasons for a tree's decline, not all of them obvious. Age itself is a primary reason. The heartwood of fruit trees is very susceptible to rot once it is exposed, and trunk rot is eventually fatal. Trunk rot is the most obvious terminal condition visible in an old tree. What is not visible is the tree's root zone, and that is where many of the ailments of old trees occur.

Drainage problems will decrease a tree's vigor because no fruit tree does well in poorly drained soil. Nemotodes, microscopic round-worms that feed off the roots, are a major problem in old orchards, especially in regions where the soil remains warm all year. Nema-todes are only detectable through expensive laboratory testing, and only soil fumigation, even more expensive, will totally eliminate these pests. Decreasing or eliminating the use of fungicides and adding compost will encourage nematode predators, thereby naturally keeping this pest under control.

In addition to poor drainage, site problems can range from poor air circulation to shading from neighboring trees. Climate is often the cause of nonproductive trees, and there is not much you can do if it is too hot or too cold to grow a particular variety. Also, fruit trees may be naturally less productive in some years than in others. Some trees are alternate bearing; that is, they bear heavily one year and little or not at all the next. This can be alleviated by fruit thinning. Unfavorable conditions for pollination are often overlooked as a reason for poor crops. Nearly all fruit species require one other variety for cross-pollination, and even if you've provided for that you are dependent on an ample supply of honeybees to do the pollinating.

Fruit trees have a biological imperative to reproduce. Often they will put out more flowers, fruit and seed if stressed. The many ills that can befall an old tree should not deter you from an attempt to restore yours. The tree has grown there for decades, and most fruit trees are remarkably tenacious. For years I cared for the rotted-out shell of an apple tree, all that was left of the last tree in a forgotten orchard. It was growing in the shade of a neighbor's spruce and was so weak it could not support itself, so I propped it up with cedar posts. The elderly widow who owned that fading tree loved it, and every year it rewarded us with flowers and fruit. Wouldn't it be worth some effort to see that old tree in your meadow yield a few more harvests?

Dormant Season Insect Control

While pruning in winter you can often spot many insect eggs. Learn to identify the good ones and the bad. On the terminals and watersprouts you will often find hundreds of aphid eggs — tiny black specks spread around the shoot. They are particularly obvious on young trees. Although you can't do much about them at this time of year, forewarned is forearmed. Prepare to use an oil spray when the buds break open, or an aphicide at petal fall.

Tent caterpillars leave a tight cluster of eggs that looks like a light brown lump of gum, the size of a nickel, wrapped around the twig. Wherever you find a "tent" in May, you will find these egg masses close by. While dormant, remove the egg mass by peeling it off the twig. My pockets are often full of these when I come in from pruning, and my trees are empty of the caterpillars in June. Throw the egg masses in the fire.

Scrape some loose scaly bark off a few trees in the winter to see if there are any codling moth cocoons. Numerous woodpecker holes are indicative of present or previous codling moth pupae. Mite eggs appear as tiny, powdery red eggs on terminals and new growth. Many of these will warn you to use an oil spray. Look especially around scars on the branches, and on the undersides of twigs which are not exposed to direct sunlight. Scale covers noticed now are dead, but under each one are eggs ready to hatch soon after petal fall. Removing a scale cover now will prevent 40 to 70 eggs from hatching. Other insects, such as apple maggot and plum curculio, overwinter underground or outside of the orchard. Spotting them in the dormant season is impossible. You will benefit by looking for the above insects, however, while you are in the trees pruning.

Dormant oil sprays have long been used by chemical and organic growers. The latter tend to use it as a sort of panacea — something relatively non-toxic that they can spray in good conscience. However, few really know what it is that they are spraying for! Dormant oil is effective against five pests: aphids, mites, scales, buffalo treehoppers and pear psylla. I'm amazed at how often I hear people swear that the oil spray cured their trees of apple worms.

Aphids and scales are somewhat deterred by delayed dormant oil sprays. "Delayed dormant" means that the highly refined oil is applied when a little green tissue is exposed in the fruit buds. Mites are seldom a problem in organic orchards, but if there is a flare-up, oil will help control the problem mites. I prefer not to use oil sprays unless there is a definite, specific need.

The exception is for young trees, up to seven to ten years old. These are especially susceptible to sucking insects which can severely stunt their growth when target insects become problems. I give these young trees a split application of superior oil - ½ the recommended rate at green tip, and seven to ten days later another ½ rate at half-inch green bud stage.

Note: Oil spray is incompatible with sulfur, and sulfur should not be applied within thirty days of a dormant oil spray. If you are relying on sulfur as a fungicide, DO NOT USE OIL.

Degree Days

Nature rebels at any attempt to match seasonal changes to a calendar. Every year is different for every region and there are too many variables to say that codling moth, for example, will hatch on May 17 every year. Most accurate predictions are based on accumulated growing degree days, often called thermal units. Degree days are estimates of plant or insect growth based on ambient temperature measurements. One degree day is accumulated for each degree above a base temperature for each day. Thus, if 40 degrees F is the base temperature, and the average temperature is 65 degrees F, 25 degree days will have accumulated during the day.

Keeping track of degree days will take much of the guesswork out of predicting your spray schedule. One can safely predict that bloom will occur when 430 degree days above 40 degrees F have accumulated. See the following chart. Plum curculio will emerge when 300 degree days have accumulated and control of this pest should begin when the 320 degree day mark is reached. The dates will vary every year, but the plants and the insects are predictable in their response to the season's ambient temperature. Using this information, and your observations in the field, you will be well on your way to developing your own schedule.

Degree Days — Nature's Calendar

Degree Days Celsius = Average temperature — Base Temperature

$$DDC = \frac{max + min}{2} - 5° \ C$$

Degree Days Fahrenheit = Average temperature — Base Temperature

$$DDF = \frac{max + min}{2} - 40° \ F$$

By keeping a running total of degree days on your calendar you can predict the approximate dates of bud stages and insect emergence. Record with the degree day totals the first sign of insect damage in your orchard.

Green Tip	65 DDC	above 5 C	Petal Fall	300 DDC	5 C
	120 DDF	40 F		540 DDF	40 F
Red Banded Leafroller	65 DDC	5 C	Codling Moth		
	120 DDF	40 F	adult emergence	300 DDC	5 C
½" Green	85 DDC	5 C		540 DDF	40 F
	150 DDF	40 F	1st eggs hatch	140 DDC	above 11 C
Gypsy Moth	85 DDC	5 C		250 DDF	50 F
	150 DDF	40 F		*after*	
Tight Cluster	125 DDC	5 C		300 DDC	above 5 C
	225 DDF	40 F		540 DDF	40 F
Pink	165 DDC	5 C	Fruit Set	350 DDC	5 C
	300 DDF	40 F		630 DDF	40 F
Plum Curculio	165 DDC	5 C	Buffalo Treehopper	350 DDC	5 C
	300 DDF	40 F		630 DDF	40 F
Bloom	240 DDC	5 C	Apple Maggot	650 DDC	5 C
	430 DDF	40 F		1170 DDF	40 F
E. Apple Sawfly	240 DDC	5 C			
	430 DDF	40 F			

Conversions:

DDC x 1.8 = DDF

DDF x .55 = DDC

Use degree day emergence data to determine
when to begin monitoring.

MARCH

- Scab — A Fungus Disease

- Fungicides — Protectant, Eradicant, and Systemic

- Organic Scab Control

- Other Diseases

- Delayed Dormant Spray

				1	2	3
				Prune and burn all black knot infections on plums and cherries.		
4	5	6	7	8	9	10
Remove tent caterpillar and other eggs.			Dormant prune peaches if valsa canker no problem. Refer to Planting Preparation in September.			
11	12	13	14	15	16	17
Fertilize when ground thaws.			Look for mite and aphid eggs, if found, prepare for oil spray.			
18	19	20	21	22	23	24
Pears bloom, Sacramento, California readers should be looking at May. Remove plastic tree guards.				Calibrate sprayers and test with water.		
25	26	27	28	29	30	31
Peach leaf curl spray, before bud break. A clean pruning cut heals the best.				Silver tip — time to graft.		

March

One of the reasons I chose orcharding over another kind of farming is that I enjoy the way that the work load is spread out over the year. There is always something to do! Although I start pruning in February when the weather is agreeable, I save the bulk of this work for March. When the sun is out and the wind is still it is a glorious time to be in the orchard.

Every tree I walk by has its own characteristics and I chuckle when I think of how, when I first started pruning, I tried to reconcile the peculiarities of my trees with the diagrams and photographs in the literature on pruning. This reminds me of the articles I've seen on building stone walls in which there are nice drawings of finished stone walls in which every stone fits perfectly. I've seen few trees that fit any perfect mold, and it's only through experience that I've learned to adapt the ideal to the reality.

I've learned to accept that when there are hundreds of trees to prune, every tree won't be perfect. I work through the orchard quickly, then go back over and touch up where necessary. Some old trees that I have worked on for years need very little work except thinning. I can do four of these an hour. Other trees that have been neglected for years can take several hours per tree.

I do most of my pruning with a short (six foot) pole saw, hand pruners, and a sharp knife. When these tools have good edges they are a pleasure to use. There is nothing that they won't cut, although I sometimes crank up the chain saw for the major limbs. I've found that the hand saw makes a much cleaner cut than heavy loppers which tend to mutilate the wood no matter how sharp they are. Everyone finds his own favorite tools and I wouldn't trade mine for the world.

I used to see a lot of tent caterpillar egg masses in the trees while pruning, although I've nearly eradicated them now. I would peel them off the twigs and put them in my pocket to dispose of in the fire. Once I forgot to clean out my pockets, only to find hundreds of caterpillars crawling through the laundry basket several days later, having hatched in the warmth of the house.

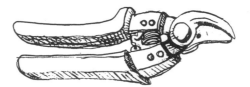

24

Scab — A Fungus Disease

Apple and pear growers know that scab is a persistent disease and difficult to control. If left uncontrolled it can actually kill young trees. It is easier to control if one understands the biology of the fungus.

Microscopic scab spores develop during the winter in the previous year's infected leaves on the ground. As soon as apple buds break open some spores will have reached maturity while other overwintering spores mature over a period of about ten weeks. The mature spores are forcibly ejected from their cases when wetted by spring rains. They are wind-borne to the branches of the trees, often over distances of up to a mile.

A dry spring, followed by a heavy rain, will result in a more heavy spore discharge because more spores will have matured during the long dry period. A spring of frequent rains will release the spores more gradually, giving more, but lighter infections.

Spores germinate on and infect developing tissues only if moisture is present for a certain length of time, the time depending on the temperature. The accompanying chart tells how soon under certain weather conditions the infection will occur. Scab takes from seven to seventeen days to become visibly detectable, depending on temperature.

To identify scab, look at the underside of the new leaves for an olive green spot three-sixteenths of an inch in diameter, darker than the rest of the leaf. The spot will darken and harden with age. In severe infections the entire leaf will be covered. The fruit is infected first in the sepal (stem) end. Look for small grey spots. Later infections will resemble the spots on the leaves.

Once you've detected scab, it's too late to do much about this primary infection except to apply some newer, systemic eradicant fungicides. But the spreading of the disease can be controlled through the timely application of regular fungicides. Secondary infections (from the spores generated by primary infections) do the most damage to fruit and foliage, so the key to reducing the amount of fungicides is to prevent the primary infections.

Scab Spore Loads — Recent experiments by plant pathologists point out the importance of knowing the relative amount of spores present in the orchard if a reduced fungicide program is to be implemented. The amount of spore inoculum (spore load) in the orchard varies from year to year and from site to site. In places where the spore load pressure is high, strict attention must be paid to the scab infection periods to be sure that foliage has dried completely before considering the infection period to have ended.

Consider the leaf at the end of a wet period. The leaf may be 90 percent dry but often a few drops of water will remain on the leaf, often near the stem end. If there is only a small amount of spore inoculum present, the chances of it being in contact with those few drops of water is less than if there were a lot of spore inoculum. The spores have to be in contact with the water to infect the tissue.

Many factors contribute to the individual orchard's spore load: the number of scab spores left over from the previous year, cultivation practices, sanitation, spores from outside the orchard and seasonal conditions.

Orchardists should examine the history of scab in their trees. Whenever possible, reduce spore loads by removing fallen leaves and fruit, removing wild or abandoned trees, and controlling secondary scab infections during the growing season. Reducing the scab spore load in the orchard will reduce the amount of times you will have to put on the foul weather gear and go out in the rain to spray your trees.

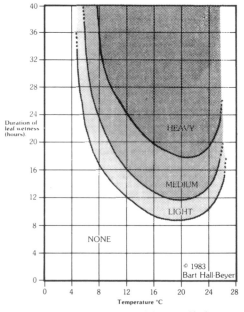

Relation of temperature and duration of leaf wetness to the severity of scab infection. In periods of intermittant rain, ten hours of sunny weather are required to stop an infection.

Fungicides — Protectant, Eradicant, and Systemic

The ability of a fungicide to control fungus infections which have already invaded plant tissue is known as "kickback." Some fungicides have almost no kickback effect. They must be applied before spores infect the leaves or fruit. Other fungicides have the ability to interrupt the process of the developing infection long after it has taken place. Still other fungicides are "systemic," i.e. they enter the vascular system of the plant and combat pre-existing infections from within.

Prediction of infection periods is difficult so without using fungicides with some kickback, one must keep preventative fungicides on the trees at all times, anticipating wet periods. This can be quite wasteful as it is possible to apply fungicides many times in anticipation of an infection period that never materializes.

Using eradicant fungicides allows growers to eliminate unnecessary sprays, to apply fungicides only when certain that an infection has occurred, and to control infections that for some reason were not treated.

Some growers are using eradicant/protectant fungicide mixes to decrease the number of fungicide applications. In this approach, a long term protectant is added to an eradicant fungicide and applied after an infection has occurred. The eradicant wipes out the existing infections and the protectant eliminates the need to spray for the following scab infection period. If you are interested in this approach, consult your state/provincial pomologist for local recommendations. Although these chemicals are more powerful than protectant fungicides, less total fungicide is added to the orchard.

Scab

Scab Infection Chart

Average Air Temperature Degrees F.*	Hours of Leaf Wetness for Infection **	Days for Secondary Spores to Develop	
32–40	48	17+	Secondary infections
40–42	30	17+	of fruit and foliage
42–45	22	17+	will occur if the
45–50	15	17	primary infections
50–53	13	16	are not controlled.
53–58	12	14	
58–62	10	9	Primary spore discharge
62–75	9	8	ends in mid June

* Add lowest and highest temperature during wet period, divide by two for average.

** This is for primary infections — secondary infections can occur in one-third less time.

1) After the start of a rain it takes 10 hours for the foliage to dry. The average temperature is 50 degrees. No infection has taken place. No need to spray.

2) A long rainy spell lasts 24 hours at a temperature of 48 degrees. If a protectant fungicide was not applied before or during this wet period, an eradicant fungicide must be used.

Eradicant Fungicide Table

Average Temp. degrees F.	Hours from start of wet period	Fungicides with kickback properties
35–40	12–24	All
	24–48	lime-sulfur, Captan, Manzate, Cyprex
	48–72	Dichlone
41–50	12	All
	12–24	lime-sulfur, Captan, Manzate, Cyprex
	24–48	Dichlone, Phygon*,
	48–72	Funginex
51 -	6	All
	6–12	Captan, Manzate, Cyprex
	12–18	Cyprex, Dichlone
	18–48	Dichlone, Phygon*
	48–72	Funginex

* Not after petal fall.

Organic Scab Control

The only current ecological, long term solution to the immense pressure of apple scab in eastern orchards is the revival of old scab-tolerant apple cultivars and the continued introduction of improved scab resistant varieties. Orchardists without these varieties must employ fungicides. If growers are committed to producing organic fruit they must resort to caustic, preventative fungicides like sulfur, lime-sulfur, bordeaux and copper.

These materials are mostly preventative, that is they have to be on the leaf when the scab spore lands in order to "burn" it. Lime-sulfur has some kickback but has phytotoxic effects if overused. This means that the organic orchardist must be aware of temperature and leaf wetness at all times during the scab season in order to make sure that there are preventative fungicides on the trees at all times. An instrument which records temperature and humidity would be an important addition in a commercial-sized organic orchard, as well as newly developed scab spore monitoring devices.

Disadvantages of these materials are that they can cause phytotoxic damage to leaves, harm various predators and parasites especially beneficial mites, diminish necessary soil fungi and possibly overload the soil with excess copper or sulfur. The degree of this disruption to the orchard eco-system depends on the quanitity of the materials used and the spraying methods. Leaf damage can be reduced by spraying caustic fungicides with a surfactant or spreader-sticker on a cool, cloudy day after a rain but before the leaves dry. Great care must be taken with dilution rates and sprayer performance. Sulfur must be agitated constantly in the sprayer to avoid settling.

Wettable sulfur is composed of elemental sulfur and bentonite clay. When it is sprayed on leaf surfaces it oxidizes to form secondary compounds which burn the scab spores when they land. Wettable sulfur is difficult to work with as it is messy, smells horrible, and can clog spray lines if not continuously agitated. No form of sulfur can be used within a month of an oil spray. Wettable sulfur is often termed "microfine" sulfur. It is the fineness of the grind that is critical because the surface area available for oxidation is more important than the total amount of sulfur used.

Recent development in liquid sulfur emulsions (not suspensions) may be the breakthrough that greatly reduces the ecological and practical disadvantage of sulfur use. THAT Flowable Sulfur and Sulcide are two new liquid sulfur products being marketed. Tests have indicated that this material can be used effectively at rates as low as 10 percent wettable sulfur by weight. Liquid sulfur is more adhesive, redistributes better and handles easier than the powder. Since less sulfur is used the environmental impact is lessened.

Lime-sulfur (calcium polysulfide) is a mixture of quicklime and sulfur. It is more caustic than sulfur and can eradicate recent scab infections. This also means that it can cause more damage. It should be used only as a last resort when scab has gotten out of control, and no sulfur-based fungicides should be used during bloom.

Bordeaux spray is a mixture of copper sulfate, hydrated lime and water. It combines the fungicidal properties of copper with the caustic properties of lime. There are a number of other copper based fungicides available including fixed copper and basic copper sulfate. These fungicides often are marketed containing synthetic ingredients unsuitable for the "organic" market. More information on their formulation is needed in order to recommend them for organic management. Homemade Bordeaux spray can be prepared by mixing eight ounces of copper sulfate in six gallons of water. After this has dissolved add a slurry of five ounces of spray lime. Stir the mixture frequently while spraying.

Some cosmetic scab damage may have to be endured by organic orchardists without scab resistant trees. These orchardists should always be ready to make cider as the unmarketable fruit can always be turned into a profit. Hopefully organic scab control products currently in the "promising" stage will soon be available.

Scab on fruit

Other Diseases

Scab is the primary disease problem of apples and pears, and learning the biology of scab will help in the understanding of other disease problems of different fruits. In general, it is best to wait until a disease is known to exist before controls are begun. Variation from location to location is great, and in general it is better not to spray unless needed. On the other hand, if a problem is known to exist in your area, take preventative measures as soon as the season begins. The best tools for minimizing the amount of fungicides needed are weather monitoring and sanitation.

Fire Blight — A bacterial disease, fire blight can be a major problem in apple and pear orchards. Once established, it is nearly impossible to eradicate, and control with streptomycin is expensive. Fire blight is spread by rain and insects during bloom. Temperatures have to be above 65 degrees, and high humidity or rain present. Incubation is four to five days, after which blossoms wilt and turn brown. Amber ooze appears on the fruit pedicel, and eventually the fruit spur and the leaves attached to it wilt and turn black. Secondary infections affect twigs, especially succulent new growth. Control fire blight by being careful not to apply too much nitrogen, especially to pears. High nitrogen levels cause excessive susceptible new growth. During bloom, monitor the blossoms to catch infections at the early stage of development. Prune off all infected parts 12 inches below the visible sign of infection. Sterilize pruners with a 1:10 bleach solution between cuts, and BURN prunings. In severe cases, consult your extension fruit specialist for streptomycin recommendations. New evidence shows that the M26 dwarfing rootstock is susceptible to fire blight.

Brown Rot — This fungus can be a serious problem of stone fruits in temperate regions. Spores are released from several sources, primarily "mummified" fruit on the tree and on the ground. The fungus enters the fruit through injuries, mechanical or insect induced. The plum curculio and oriental fruit moth are principal culprits in spreading this disease. Symptoms include blossom and twig blight, and fruit rot. Blossom blight is a grey-brown discoloration and decay. Twig blight infections are sunken, brown, elliptical cankers. Fruit becomes progressively more susceptible later in the season, so early stages should be controlled. Meticulously clean up and burn all mummified fruit from the ground and from the trees. In extreme cases, fungicides should be applied during bloom and at petal fall.

Black Knot — Plum and cherry trees are severely injured by this fungus, which girdles branches with lumpy black growths. The new infections appear in late summer as long, soft, greenish swellings that often have a pink mold associated. The second year the infections harden into dark knots. Eventually the knots girdle the branch or trunk. Infected trees, wild or cultivated, which are severely infected must be cut and burned to stop the spread of the disease. In minor cases the infected parts can be pruned out and burned.

Black Knot of plums, cherries, and peaches

Cedar Rust — Some new varieties are resistant to this disease, which has an alternate host of the red cedar species. Wherever possible, the red cedars should be removed for one half mile around the orchard. Polyram is effective in a preventive program.

Powdery Mildew — Suspect this fungus whenever you see a white powdery growth on watersprouts, new leaves, and twigs early in the season. Prune out infected parts. Regular applications of sulfur are effective in controlling severe infections.

Leaf Spot — Cherries and plums can be defoliated by this fungus, sometimes called the "shot-hole" fungus because of the holes that it leaves in foliage. The first sign of the disease is tiny purple lesions on the upper surface of the leaves, about seven to ten days after petal fall. Cyprex is the preferred fungicide.

Valsa Canker — Sometimes called cytospora canker, is a fungus that invades peach woody parts through injuries, pruning cuts, or other breaks in the bark. Pruning should be delayed until buds are open, as earlier pruning cuts are entry points for the disease. Symptoms are wilting and browning of new shoots. Older cankers are black, torn callous tissue, often covered with oozing sores. Besides late pruning, cultivation practices which encourage winter hardiness, insect control, and cultivation will help keep this disease in check.

Black Rot — Black rot, also called frogeye leaf-spot because of its characteristic mark on the leaf, is a serious fungus disease if it becomes established in the apple orchard. It affects leaves and woody parts of the tree as well as fruit. Often fruit with black rot will remain on the tree as shriveled-up "mummies." If you have any of these mummies on your trees, or on neighboring, uncared-for trees, begin a strict program of sanitation. Dispose of infected fruit in sealed plastic bags as soon as the disease is detected. Burn all prunings, and consider using a mild fungicide on summer pruning cuts or wounds. Burn all dead wood, and keep a clean orchard.

All diseases can be controlled without chemicals by interrupting their life cycle in the spore-forming stage. This involved constant vigilance and cleaning up disease sources. Once the source of spores is taken away the disease will usually cease to be a problem.

Delayed Dormant Spray

Bud Stages: Silver Tip, Green Tip, Half-inch Green

Insect Pest	Organic Control	Chemical Control
Mites Aphids Scales Psylla	superior oil — split sprays one half at green tip, one-half at tight cluster or full dose at one-half inch green	none needed

Disease	Organic Control	
Scab	sulfur, except not within 30 days of oil. Bordeaux	Pre-infection: Polyram Post-infection: see eradicant table (March)
Powdery mildew Brown rot (cherries)	sulfur, except as above cultivate, remove all mummified fruit	

Fertilizers		
All trees	apply compost early foliar feed at one-half inch green for known deficiencies	

See November for pesticide rates.

APRIL

- Sprayers

- The First Spray

- Foliar Fertilization

- Pesticides — What Not to Use

- Beneficial Insects and Mites

- Pre-Bloom Spray

				1	2	3
				Observe fruit buds for green tip.	Start grafting.	
4	5	6	7	8	9	10
Scab sprays may start with first green tissue.				Peaches bloom in Virginia. Arrange for bees for pollination.		
11	12	13	14	15	16	17
Cherries bloom in California. Watch for tent caterpillars. Warm rains bring severe scab.				Delayed dormant superior oil spray at half-inch green bud. Apples bloom in Illinois.		
18	19	20	21	22	23	24
Warning — if you use oil you cannot use sulfur for thirty days.				Winter injury — peeling or cracked bark: paint with white latex.		
25	26	27	28	29	30	
Prune peaches in valsa canker regions; paint or spray pruning cuts.				Hang sawfly/plant bug traps at pink bud stage.		

April

After the equinox life in the orchard quickens. I begin walking through the trees daily, looking for signs of swelling buds. Every variety starts at a different time, and I look through my old records to see what to expect. I start keeping track of the weather in April, and the comparison over the years has been very helpful. This year looks as if it could be a week to ten days behind last year, which is good news. I still have to put new gaskets on one of my sprayers.

This is the time to take stock of winter injury, although true winterkill (freezing injury) will not be evident for two or three months. I check around the base of each tree for rodent damage, and I inspect the trunks of the trees for bark splitting. I like to carry colored ribbon with me to mark those trees that need wound dressing. I know the trees well enough to remember which ones need attention, but I also know that marking the trees will speed up the process of treatment, and this time of year speed and efficiency are important.

It looks as if the buds of the Liberty trees are furthest along this year. This new disease resistant variety is an early bloomer, yet I look at the development of its buds with a calmness that comes from knowing that I'm not going to have to spray it for scab. The Macspur trees, also with rapidly swelling buds, are the ones I am going to have to worry about first. As soon as the buds break and expose green tissue it is susceptible to scab infections. Then I am going to have to monitor the weather even more closely.

Soon, when the temperature is high enough, and the foliage is wet long enough, I will put on the foul weather gear, the rubber boots, the respirator, and the goggles. I'll load up the sprayer with the appropriate fungicide for the occasion and get it on the trees. It's not a pleasant chore, but I know that by spraying only when necessary I can keep fungicides to a minimum. As I walk past the rows of disease resistant varieties I feel a calm satisfaction that they will be scab free without my having to mess with sprays.

Sprayers

Whether your orchard is organic or chemical, you will need a good quality sprayer to care for your trees. There simply is no way around it — fruit trees need to be sprayed, whether with seaweed extract or with Guthion. Sprayers enable the orchardist to apply foliar fertilizers and biodynamic soil preparations as well as pesticides. Choosing the correct sprayer for your orchard is an important commitment to proper management.

The sprayer is essential for the orchardist as the combine is to the wheat farmer, the cultivator to the vegetable grower, or the hay machinery to the dairy farmer. The equipment has to work well when you need it and any failure during the season can be disastrous. Make sure that the sprayer is cleaned up well at the end of the season and check it out again in the early spring. Make sure that you have plenty of spare gaskets, hoses, and other spare parts on hand. Pay special attention to the air cleaner and take the time to run a compression test. You don't want to be doing a ring job in May. Hours count with those first scab infections. Be ready.

Think big — spraying can get to be a real chore, and if the sprayer is undersized, the chore can be so unpleasant that it doesn't get done. There are many types of sprayers available, and one must choose carefully the type that best fits the particular situation. Here is a brief rundown on some sprayer categories:

Sprayers and Their Applications

Type of Sprayer	Capacity	Practical Number of trees (standard)	Tank agitation	Advantages	Disadvantages
hand-held compression	1–3 gal.	1–5	No	Price Simplicity	Manual agitation, weight, difficult to get high branches, clogging
back pack manual pump	3–5 gal.	1–12	No	Price simplicity	weight, need to refill often
back pack power mister	3 gal.	3–20	Yes	Thorough coverage	Noisy, need to refill often, causes drift
self-contained hydraulic pump and tank (trailer)	50–100 gal.	10–200	Yes	Good coverage, can be towed behind vehicle	Hand-held gun requires frequent moving of unit along rows
pto hydraulic pump	50–300 gal.	20–500	Yes	Tractor powered	Same
pto mister	100–500 gal.	> 100	Yes	Continuous operation	Precautions needed to avoid drift

The First Spray

Before running the sprayer, check the machinery to see that the fuel system has been drained properly and that everything is greased up. Put in some fresh fuel, kick over the engine, and when everything is running smoothly, pump some fresh water through. Check for leaks in the system, look for worn or frayed places on hoses, and be sure that shut-off valves and other safety features are working properly. Run the sprayer long enough to be sure it will work when you need it.

Measure the volume of your sprayer so that you can mix accurate proportions for your container. You will need accurate measuring devices to mix correctly. All tools which contact poisons need to be locked away from children and clearly marked "Not For Food — Poison." To calibrate the amount of spray your rig delivers, measure the amount of water it takes to refill the tank after spraying water for ten minutes. Divide that volume by ten to figure how much your sprayer sprays per minute. With this information, you can accurately apply sprays at the appropriate rates by spraying for a given amount of time.

The first spray should be with something non-toxic such as sea-weed extract, so that you can learn the peculiarities of your sprayer, your route through the orchard, and your individual trees before applying toxic materials. Application rates depend upon the target, and a mature tree with full foliage is a much different target than a young tree in bud. The recommended rates are for diluted sprays, applied to the point of run-off from the trees. Tree Row Volume (TRV) is a new system of calculating spray rates for varying tree size and spacing. It is being used increasingly by commercial orchardists. The amount of space that trees actually occupy in an acre is calculated and used as a factor in determining the spray rate. Refer to the February and March '86 American Fruit Grower for a discussion of this method of sprayer calibration.

The spray applicator has to constantly ask himself the question: Where does the spray go? What proportion is reaching the target, how much is drifting, how does the spray enter the environment? One of the reasons I don't like to spray poisons is that I cannot account for 100 percent of the spray, or its long term effects on non-target organisms. Learning to use your sprayer as carefully and as effectively as possible will be the result of this kind of aware questioning. WEAR PROTECTIVE CLOTHING   READ THE LABELS

Foliar Fertilization

Foliar fertilization is the spraying of minerals on the leaf surface, their absorption and subsequent translocation in the plant. The best long term method of fertilization is feeding the soil rather than the plant. A fertile soil will supply an optimum balanced amount of nutrients to the tree. If a fertile soil has not been achieved, or because of certain climatic, rootstock or soil situations, the direct feeding of a plant may be necessary. For example: applications of limestone may have tied up available boron, nitrogen release may be delayed by a long cold spring, a rootstock may not be able to absorb certain nutrients, alkaline soil may hinder mineral flow to the roots, or a leaf analysis may turn up a surprise zinc deficiency.

In these cases foliar fertilization can help correct the problem. Leaves can absorb minerals through the cuticle but only in limited quantities. It is therefore unfeasible to try to supply significant amounts of major nutrients through the leaves. Any excess will just burn the leaves (phytotoxicity). This fact led many researchers to state that foliar fertilization was ineffective. However, orchardists have been leaders in the sprayer technology of foliar fertilization. For years fruit growers have been foliar feeding effectively to supplement their soil programs. In the northeast orchardists have been using boron, magnesium and nitrogen while in the west they have sprayed zinc, maganese and iron.

Absorption and translocation of foliar nutrients depends on ambient temperature, light levels, surface pH, energy availability and leaf surface moisture. Some minerals (calcium and boron) are easily absorbed but poorly translocated while others (iron and copper) move quickly once in the plant but have difficulty passing through the leaf cuticle.

The chelation of some mineral salts has greatly increased their effectiveness. Chelation is a process which binds minerals into an organic molecular structure. This enables the mineral to be absorbed and translocated more easily. Liquid seaweed extract has been popular with organic orchardists. The seaweed or kelp plant itself illustrates the principle of foliar feeding because it is anchored to the sea bed by holdfasts not roots and feeds through its leaves from the mineral-rich ocean. Since it balances and chelates these nutrients its cell sap extract has become a useful foliar material. As well as being a broad range trace mineral spray it contains growth hormones including cytokinins which activate plant enzyme systems and increase cell division.

The effectiveness of foliar sprays depends on the material used, timing, sprayer technology, and knowledge of leaf surface chemistry. In practical terms spraying is most effective in the early hours of a cloudy humid day. The use of a surfactant, which de-ionizes the leaf surface and enables the spray material to cling, and a sprayer which delivers a mist of fine droplets is important. It is also essential to time the delivery of nutrients or hormones to match the stage of plant growth where they are required.

Foliar fertilization should be approached carefully with the understanding that it only supplements, often temporarily, a soil fertility program. For example when northeast orchardists stopped liming regularly (on bad advice) it took a few years before calcium deficiencies started to show up as storage breakdown, bitter pit, etc. Then orchardists were forced to spray, at some expense, calcium chloride or chelated calcium until limestone applications could be absorbed by the soil.

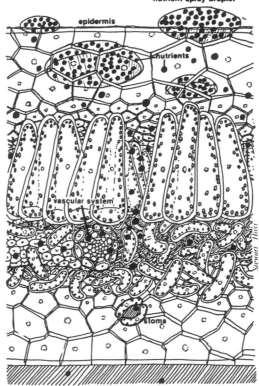

Cross-section of a leaf

Pesticides — What Not to Use

Spraying is a necessary function of orcharding, but good orchard management means reducing the amount of sprays and being selective about the pesticides used. Apples are the most heavily sprayed food in North America — they receive more pesticides per acre than corn, citrus or any other pesticide-managed crop.

Home fruit growers have long relied on "all purpose orchard spray" to control their pest problems. All purpose spray, marketed under several names, can wreak havoc with beneficial insects and is a wasteful attempt by chemical companies to simplify spraying. It is tempting to think that one product can do it all but this is not the case.

These mixtures are usually a combination of a fungicide such as Captan and several inexpensive broad-spectrum insecticides such as Malalathion and Methoxychlor. As will become evident in using the spray recommendations in this almanac, fungicides and insecticides should never be mixed without specific knowledge indicating a need. There are many times during the season when a fungicide is needed and not an insecticide, or vice versa. Combining the two is wasteful, expensive and harmful to the beneficial species that you want to encourage.

Often users of all-purpose spray find that they need to supplement with an aphicide or miticide. The insecticides in the all-purpose spray are non-selective and the natural predators of aphids and mites are killed. One advertisement lists over 20 pests that are killed by their product. They do not list the nearly 100 non-pest species that are wiped out. The orchardist who really wants to minimize his efforts will take every precaution to utilize the existing natural controls. Initially it will take a little more effort to select appropriate pesticides according to the season and the needs, but in the long run it is more economic and safer for the applicator and the environment.

Captan is a dangerous chemical. Relatively low in toxicity (see November) it has been known to be a potent mutagen since 1975. It is also considered a potential carcinogen, especially if Captan dust is inhaled. The cancer-causing complications, especially in combination with other chemicals, are not fully known yet. DO NOT USE CAPTAN WITHOUT A RESPIRATOR.

Beneficial Insects and Mites

Over 95 percent of the insects and mites found in the orchard do not harm the fruit crop. In fact many of them perform beneficial tasks including pest control and pollination.

The predators and parasites of orchard pests are a key component of ecological pest control. These beneficials may already be present in the orchard, can be collected from the surrounding area or may be ordered from insectiaries. These predators and parasites will be effective if pesticides harmful to them are not used, their prey is present in sufficient numbers and a supplemental feeding program is provided.

Predators and parasites will naturally appear when pesticide spraying is stopped or greatly reduced. They may not establish control over all pests quickly enough to satisfy the economic need of the grower. As part of a transition program from chemical to natural controls an orchardist may have to import beneficial species. Orchardists may be able to gather natural enemies in the form of egg cases, larvae or adults from unsprayed orchards. For example, the predatory gall midge and syrphid fly larvae are frequently found feeding on aphids in the sheltered curled portion of leaves in unsprayed orchards or wild trees. These, and other beneficials can be collected in a ventilated box and introduced into the orchard.

The major predators and parasites available from insectiaries include trichogramma wasps, ladybird beetles, green lacewings, and predatory mites.

Trichogramma wasps parasitize the eggs of over 200 insect pests including codling moth, gypsy moth, and fruitworms. Most insectiaries recommend their release into the orchard three times during the season at two week intervals. The well known adult ladybird beetle, and its lesser known but more voracious larvae stage, is an aphid and mite predator. Both the larval and adult stage of the green lacewing are predators of aphids, caterpillars and other soft-bodied insects and spider mites.

Predatory mites available from insectiaries can control smaller pest mites under most conditions. These mites are larger than pest mites and feed on European red mite, apple rust mite and two-spotted mite. Mites can also be raised by the orchardist with access to a greenhouse facility. Insectiaries can supply detailed information on the care and nurture of these beneficials as well as release schedules.

One of the major reasons for the failure of imported beneficial species is the lack of a food supply attractive to them. Orchardists must supply alternate food sources for these beneficials. The insectiaries can usually supply a feeding supplement ("artificial honeydew") with the insect order. An example is Wheast, a high protein by-product of the cheese industry. This can be easily set out in feeding stations to carry over the predators when pest populations are low.

The orchard ecosystem can be structured so that it provides for the needs of its beneficials. Buckwheat can be planted in various plots around the orchard each year. The flowers provide a food source for bees, syrphid flies (hoverflies) and other beneficials. Dill or other umbelliferae can be rotated with buckwheat and clover in plots spaced throughout the orchard. Umbelliferous plants with exposed nectaries accessible to small wasps have proved to be the best food source for these parsitic wasps. Perennial plantings should include wild parsnip, Queen Anne's Lace and caraway. A poly-crop system will help create an ecologically diverse orchard that supports biological control.

Pre-Bloom Spray

Bud Stages: Tight Cluster, Pink, Bloom

Note: control insects only when traps indicate thresholds are crossed.

Insect Pest	Organic Control	Chemical Control
Tent caterpillar	Remove manually, or spot-spray Bt	Spot-spray Imidan before bloom
Tarnished plant bug European apple sawfly	Observe traps weekly, record weekly catches	None needed yet
Leafminers, winter moth	Bacillus thuringiensis	No insecticides In Bloom!!!
Eye-spotted bud moth	Observe traps	
Aphids	No control needed at this time.	

Disease		
Scab	*Sulfur Bordeaux table (March)	Pre-infection: Polyram Post-infection: see eradicant
Fire blight	Prune, disinfect tools bloom	"TOP COP" (Stoller) with sulfur at 10%
Powdery mildew	*Sulfur	
Brown rot (cherries)	Cultivate, remove all mummified fruit; sulfur	
Black knot	*Sulfur	Polyram or Phygon

* Do not use sulfur within thirty days of oil

Fertilizers		
All trees	Apply compost early Foliar feed at early pink	

See November for pesticide rates.

MAY

- Bees in the Orchard
- Insect Monitoring Traps
- Early Season Insect Pests
- Mites
- Post-Bloom Spray.

During bloom, identify nearby wild trees to be removed. Cultivate and mow before bloom. Watch for fire blight at bloom. Cherries bloom in Ohio.			**1**	**2**	**3**	
4	**5**	**6**	**7**	**8**	**9**	**10**
Check new shoots of peach and plum: oriental fruit moth.				Nutrient sprays at early pink and at petal fall.		
11	**12**	**13**	**14**	**15**	**16**	**17**
Hang codling moth traps. Renew pheromone capsules every 10 days. Check for leaf miner.				Record dates of bloom for all varieties.		
18	**19**	**20**	**21**	**22**	**23**	**24**
Hang cherry maggot traps. Remove blossoms, fruit from central leader of trees.				Apples bloom in Nova Scotia. Check for curculio feeding when temperature above 70.		
25	**26**	**27**	**28**	**29**	**30**	**31**
Cultivate under peaches to discourage brown rot.				Monitor for scales at petal fall. Tired of scab sprays? Plant disease immune varieties.		

May

The orchard in bloom is a wonderful treat for all the senses. I take my time walking through the orchard today, stopping to inspect the clustered flowers and buds, filling my nostrils with the sweet aroma, all the while listening to the crescendo of the honeybees as they go about their work. As I come to one of the tall, slender crabapples I have planted for pollinating, I stop to look at the bees. They are crowded onto this tree, flitting from blossom to blossom, unconcerned with my presence.

Looking closely I can see that to get to the nectar which they need to feed their new brood, the bees push past the pollen-laden stamens getting thoroughly covered with pollen in the process. Then they fly on to another blossom, and another, and eventually on to another tree. There they will repeat the procedure, picking up more pollen and depositing a few grains as well — enough to fertilize another variety's blossom.

Because I keep my own bees this process has the additional reward of supplying delicious honey for my table but I have to be careful. Honeybees are very sensitive to pesticides and I take precautions not to expose them to any. I use no insecticides while the orchard is in bloom, and I am careful to keep the orchard well mowed all the time so that the bees do not get in the habit of foraging in the orchard cover. If there is any chance that the bees might be exposed to a spray, I can cover the hive with netting to keep them in while I spray but I haven't had to do this in years. The bees have learned to forage elsewhere when the orchard is not in bloom and I have learned not to use toxic sprays when any plants are in bloom.

I'm also aware of other insect life on the trees now — traps have picked up some sawflies and close examination of some young leaves reveals the "mines" of leafminers. Neither of these pests has caused significant damage to the crop in the past and I'm not going to worry about them this year. I know that by spraying for them I will be harming beneficial species that are the natural controls which keep these insects in balance. The really tough pests are just around the corner and bloom is the time to prepare for them. Plum curculio are making their way from the woodlot back to the orchard, first to the ground cover under the drip line perimeter of the trees where they remain for a week or so before going up into the trees. Sometimes, if I'm lucky, by putting my ear near the ground I can hear one of them making a singing noise which they use to bring new arrivals together, possibly so that they can mate. I wonder if chickens can hear them better than I can and that if I could keep some under the trees at this time they might carry out the bulk of the pest removal program for me.

Bees in the Orchard

Orchardists who keep bees need to protect the hives when insecticides are used. Most commercial orchards use so many pesticides they can't possibly keep bees around. They rent hives of bees to assist pollination and are obligated not to use insecticides while the rented bees are in the orchard. The bees have to be gone before the crucial petal fall spray. I have found that with some extra precautions to protect the bees and with a natural pest control sytem, I can keep my hives near the orchard where they belong. Keeping bees has convinced me that the wonders of the insect world need a lot more respect than the senseless overspraying of the past century.

Never use insecticides when the trees or the groundcovers are in bloom. Whether the flowers are apple blossoms, clover, dandelions or goldenrod, pollinating insects will be devasted by insecticides. Bees that pick up insecticides with the pollen they carry back to the hive poison the entire hive. Whenever insecticides are used flowering groundcovers must be mowed and desirable flowering plants (buckwheat and umbelliferae) planted away from spray drift.

Spray insecticides in the late afternoon after bees have returned to their hives. Many pests are nocturnal, whereas pollinators work in the daytime. Cloudy weather is also a time when bees are less likely to be in the orchard. I keep my hives in the shade, give each one a top-waterer, and cover them with loose-fitting burlap covers whenever I need to spray an insecticide. If there are puddles in the orchard from which the bees could pick up insecticides, I make sure to keep their water supply full and try to drain the puddles. Some beekeepers feed their bees supplementary pollen and syrup during the period of covering, but the bees don't seem to take the syrup.

Beekeeping is a hobby that I am unwilling to sacrifice for the sake of pesticides. In fact, keeping bees forces me to be conscious of and careful with pesticides and I am constantly seeking ways to eliminate them entirely. Then the orchard and apiary will both thrive in a natural alliance.

Insect Monitoring Traps

In the past few years the techonology for trapping insects with visual and chemical attractants has given non-entomologists the capability to monitor emergences of many orchard pests. This ability to monitor insect emergence and populations has made it possible to time pesticide sprays for maximum effect and even to eliminate some pesticides entirely. No single factor has been more important to those wanting to reduce sprays than the development of effective insect traps. There are two types of insect traps: pheromone traps, which use chemical attractants, and visual traps.

Insects are attracted to various wavelengths of infrared. Pheromones are chemicals which insects sense not by smell as we know it, but by detecting the alteration of infrared radiation caused by the chemical. Pheromones mimic the chemical lures that female insects produce to attract males. These man-made chemical lures are very specific to each species. Pheromone traps are like beacons of invisible light for lusty male insects which get ensnared in the sticky traps.

Pheromone traps are available for many different orchard pests and other insects. They come in many different styles but the basic idea is the same. The trap consists of a sticky coated plate on which a capsule of the pheromone chemical is placed. The capsule is usually replaced every ten days or so and the sticky substance refreshed when necessary. A water-shedding cover completes the simple trap.

Suppliers furnish complete instructions with their products. Placement, replacement and specific directions will vary with different traps. Timing trap placement is a matter of experience, but keeping track of accumulated degree days will help you determine when to hang the pheromone traps. Likewise, determining the "threshold" number of insect captures which determines whether or not you spray is a matter of individual experience and needs.

Visual traps aid in attracting, trapping and controlling several insects. Tarnished Plant Bug and European Apple Sawfly are attracted to zinc-oxide white rectangles, 15cm x 20cm, hung in the trees. Covered with tanglefoot stickum the traps catch insects landing on what they perceive to be big bright leaves. Sawfly traps should be hung at eye level or a little higher on the south sides of trees at the early pink bud stage. Commercial orchardists consider four flies per trap to be the spray threshold. Plant bug traps are placed thigh-high on perimeter trees. Five adult plant bugs is the threshold for this pest.

Since plant bugs cause only superficial damage home orchardists may choose not to spray except in extreme cases. These white rectangles catch a lot of other insects as well as the target species, giving a good general idea of insect emergence.

Apple Maggot flies (July) are probably the easiest insects to catch with visual traps. In unsprayed orchards the emergent flies are attracted to bright yellow rectangles, eight inches by ten inches, which mimic the wavelength of foliage on which the flies feed before mating and laying their eggs in the fruit. In sprayed orchards, the flies seem to be more aggressive, ready to lay eggs almost immediately after emergence. In this case they are better trapped on three inch diameter dark red spheres covered with Tanglefoot. These spheres trap the females as they jump from fruit to fruit in search of a suitable place to lay their eggs. Ron Prokopy, entomologist at the University of Massachusetts, has achieved over 90 percent control of apple maggots in his test orchard using six sphere traps per tree. These traps are inexpensive, reusable and very effective against the ever-present apple maggots.

Placement of the red ball traps is critical. They should be placed about eye level in the trees, near clusters of fruit but with about twelve inches to sixteen inches of clearance between the trap and adjacent foliage. In other words, the traps must stand apart from the nearby foliage but be close enough to other fruit to attract the flies.

There are several new developments in insect trapping being studied now. The May 1985 issue of the newsletter, "IPM Practitioner" reports that several low-cost codling moth traps are being tested. Further research in pheromone technology and competition in the developing industry will soon make insect trapping easy and inexpensive.

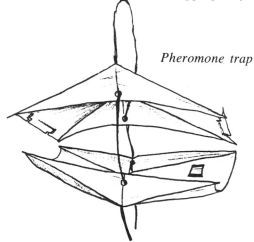

Pheromone trap

Pheromone traps are available for many insects,

Peachtree Borer	Fruittree Leafroller	Spotted Tentiform Leafminer
Codling Moth	Lesser Peachtree Borer	Tufted Apple Budmoth
Gypsy Moth	Peach Twig Borer	San Jose Scale
Obliquebanded Leafroller	Plum Fruit Moth	Oriental Fruit Moth
Eyespotted Budmoth	Green Fruitworm	Red-Banded Leafroller
	Mediterranean Fruit Fly	

Placement of insect traps is critical to good monitoring results.

Early Season Insect Pests

Insects emerge in an orderly progression as the season grows warmer. This is the time to be vigilant on your walks through the orchard. Some insects, such as the tent caterpillars, are obvious and control is easy. Others, like leaf rollers, can be trapped with pheromones and seldom pose a serious threat. Some common pests to watch for before and during bloom are:

Tent Caterpillars — Remove the egg masses in the winter. The webs of these worms are highly visible. As soon as the nests become visible prune them out and burn them, or spot spray them. Bacillus thuringiensis (B.t.) will give some control. Do not burn the nests with a torch as many of the caterpillars will drop to the ground and survive.

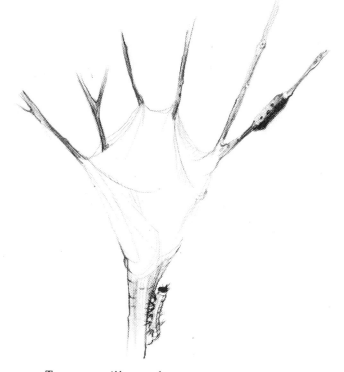

Tent caterpillar and egg mass on twig

Tarnished Plant Bug (TPB), European Apple Sawfly (EAS) — These two pests feed on buds and developing fruit. The TPB is one-quarter inch long with mottled markings of yellow, brown and black. There is a distinctive yellow triangle on either side of the body. Sanitation is the best control of this pest. The EAS is a little larger than a housefly, with numerous transverse stripes. Their mark on the fruit is distinctive: a curving, roughened scar. Both these insects can be trapped on sticky white rectangle traps. Placing these traps in the trees at the green tip stage will give some direct control and at least a good indication if more direct control will be needed.

Green Fruitworms — These are the larvae of moths. They feed on immature fruit, sometimes causing severe fruit drop and heavy scarring of fruit that remains on the trees. The moths may be trapped with a pheromone trap and controlled with Bt before bloom and at petal fall.

Spotted Tentiform Leafminer — These have become a problem where excessive insecticides killed their natural predators. During bloom look at interior leaves, holding them up against the sky. Looking through the leaf you will see a big brown spot and/or a light green or whitish area where the interior cells of the leaf have been "mined." Check twice a week for these first generation miners. Bt is somewhat effective if applied several times while the larvae are actively feeding. Pheromone traps are available for the spotted tentiform leafminer.

Red-Banded Leaf Roller — First generation larvae of this moth feed on leaves and spin fine webs. Second generation larvae hatching in July, chew grooves in the surface of the fruit. The moth has a mottled reddish-brown color with a reddish band across the wings. It can be captured in a pheromone trap and direct control can be achieved with one trap per tree. Bt will give some control as will introduced trichogramma wasps.

Scales — These sucking insects are usually found on twigs and branches. In heavy infestations a branch can be covered with these scales and weakened or killed. Except for a brief stage in its life the scale is immobile but they can be carried around like aphids by ants. Controlling ants will help, as will a delayed dormant superior oil spray.

Scale Monitoring — Bart Hall-Beyer has recommended a scale monitoring trick that he uses in order to time control sprays accurately. First he wraps black electrical tape around the branch on which scale covers have been discovered. This is coated with a thin coat of petroleum jelly. The newly emergent scale "crawlers," pale yellow grey, are easy to spot against the black background of the tape. From the time of emergence, there are only three days before a waxy covering develops on the scale crawlers, greatly increasing their protection against pesticides. Look for this mobile, vulnerable stage beginning at petal fall.

All of these pests can be tolerated to some degree depending upon the commercial requirements of the orchard. Seldom do homeowners need to spray to control these minor insects. Don't assume there is a problem until a severe flareup in population threatens the crop. At the same time, keep your eyes open as you walk through the orchard and learn to know when and how to look for these pests.

Mites

There are several species of mites which damage fruit tree foliage. European red mites and two-spotted mites are the principal villains. There are many more species of mites, most being beneficial species that keep pest mites under control. Mites are seldom a problem in well managed orchards because selective chemicals are easy on the beneficial predator species. Only when excessive amounts of non-selective insecticides are used do mites build up to damaging levels. For this reason, mites are used as indicators of mismanagement by overspraying with broad-spectrum chemicals such as synthetic pyrethroids.

Life Cycle — Eggs of pest mites overwinter on branches and twigs. Hatching begins at tight cluster, and peaks at bloom. By mid June eggs have been laid and the adult population drops off. Then in July the populations increase again. The early generation sometimes interferes with fruit bud formation resulting in less bloom the following year. The second generation damages the foliage, weakening the tree. Beneficial predator mites hatch later than pest species, and climb up the trees from their overwintering places on the ground.

Identification — Mites are tiny spider-like creatures, not insects. They feed on the undersides of leaves. With a 10x or 20x hand lens, they can be identified as pest or beneficial. By sapping the juices of the leaves, pest mites interfere with the photosynthesis process leaving reddened or "bronzed" foliage. When bronzing is noticed, it is too late for effective control in the current season.

Monitoring — Mite populations can become a problem in hot, dry weather. Seldom are the buildups uniform throughout the orchard — they tend to occur on individual trees. Look for the characteristic bronzing of the foliage. Sample 20 to 30 leaves from a suspect tree. In June up to 40 mites per leaf is acceptable. In July the numbers should drop to 10 and stay at 10 per leaf through August. Another way to predict mite problems is to look for their reddish eggs on terminal branches while pruning in the dormant season.

Organic Controls — There are enough natural predators of mites to keep them under control in most cases, especially in orchards where chemicals are used sparingly. Sulfur is definitely damaging to beneficial predatory mites. If your orchard has a history of mite damage, or if you identify particular trees as having problems, use an oil spray. Superior oil, applied at half-inch green or tight cluster (delayed dormant) is a safe effective control against mites.

Chemical Controls — In severe outbreaks of mites which cannot be controlled with oil, consult your extension pomologist for recommended miticides. Chemical miticides are very expensive, and recommendations vary in different states and provinces.

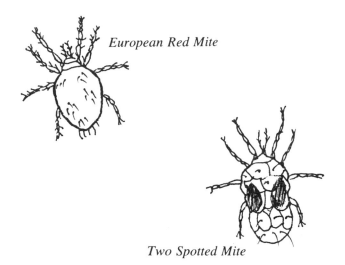

European Red Mite

Two Spotted Mite

Post-Bloom Spray

Note: control insects only when traps indicate thresholds are crossed.

Petal Fall (75% Flowers Gone)

Insect Pest	Organic Control	Chemical Control
(Note: control only when monitoring shows evidence)		
Plum curculio	Triple-plus	Imidan
Codling moth	Bt with bait	Imidan according to
Ryania with bait		to trap data
	Trichogramma release	
Leafroller	**Bt**	Not necessary
Plant bug	**Triple-Plus**	In severe cases use Imidan

Disease

(Note: observe weather to time scab sprays accordingly)

Scab	Sulfur	Pre-infection:
	Bordeaux	Polyram
		Post-infection:
		see eradicant
		table (March)
Powdery mildew	Sulfur	
Brown rot (cherries)	Cultivate, remove all mummified fruit; sulfur	
Black knot	Sulfur	Polyram or Phygon
Fire blight	Prune, disinfect tools	Streptomycin — consult extension agent "TOP COP" with sulfur

Fertilizers

All trees	No more compost
	Foliar feed all trees at petal fall especially boron and magnesium according to leaf analysis.

See November for pesticide rates.

JUNE

- Plum Curculio

- Codling Moth Other Mid-season Pests

- Fruit Thinning

- First Cover Spray

- Summer Sprays

				1	2	3
Prune apples lightly two weeks after bloom. Thin fruit before it is the size of a walnut. Cherry maggot peak. Refer to Special Care for Young Trees in August.						
4	5	6	7	8	9	10
Check for codling moth frass in blossom ends. Look for curculio and leaf-miner feeding while thinning fruit Hang apple maggot traps.						
11	12	13	14	15	16	17
Send unknown insects to state/provincial entomology lab for identification. Renew stickum on traps. Mulch all trees, especially peach. End fertilization.						
18	19	20	21	22	23	24
Remove all early drops, check for curculio, fruitworm. Remove peach watersprouts, paint wounds.						
25	26	27	28	29	30	
Hand thin apples, plums, especially peaches. Mow, cultivate, and mulch. Over 90% of fruit in which curculio eggs were laid drop to the ground now.						

57

June

June is a time of rapid growth for the trees, for the fruit, and for the burgeoning populations of insects. This is when the trees need the optimum amount of nutrients. I take note of any abnormalities in leaf size and color as I walk through the orchard now. If I can identify deficiencies I'll supplement the normal fertilization program with the appropriate foliar material. Usually I find that the staple ration of hay mulch supplies most of the nutrients my trees need, with a light dose of boron and magnesium as supplements. I take a hay fork to turn the mulch as I go down the rows, keeping it from compacting. It always amazes me how friable the soil is under a mulch and how quickly the soil life turns the straw into humus.

Much of my time in the orchard this month is spent looking for the signs of insects and disease. I carry my hand lens and my hand pruners all the time. As I prune off the tender watersprouts I check them for signs of mildew and burn the prunings if it is apparent. I look at the developing fruit clusters with the pea-sized swollen ovaries that will become fruit. It is evident now which blossoms were fertilized and which were not, the latter withering and dropping. What I'm looking for are signs of feeding by the curculio beetles, one of the toughest bugs to control organically. I recall the first time I met one of these critters face-to-face. It was sitting right on the fruit cluster, looking just as ugly as in the pictures only smaller than I had imagined. True to expectations, when I knocked it off the tree into my hand it rolled belly up and played possum. I still have the little beast in a tiny box.

The problem with curculio is that they have few if any natural predators and in areas where populations are high there is no recourse but to use an insecticide, and a powerful one at that. I'm in a borderline location where the "curcs" don't wipe out the entire crop, but some years they cause a lot of damage and fruit drop. Every year I wrestle with the decision to spray or not to spray, and if I decide to spray I want to get the timing perfect. That is why I take this daily walk so that I can find the first feeding scars which are the sign that this nemesis is back in my orchard.

58

Plum Curculio

The curculio beetles are major pests that cause significant damage to apples, plums and cherries. They feed primarily on foliage and fruit but the major damage is caused by egg-laying in the fruit. Most fruit infested with curculio eggs drop from the trees. Fruit damaged by feeding scars may remain on the tree but cannot be sold at top grade.

Life Cycle — Most adult beetles overwinter near the orchard under leaves and trash in neighboring woodlots. Some remain in the orchard but they are susceptible to cold and many perish in cold winters. Beetles emerge from dormancy gradually in May and June, peaking around petal fall for apples. Mating commences once they arrive in the orchard. Numbers remain high in June then decline in July.

As soon as the fruit is the size of a pea, egg laying commences and continues into July. Each female can lay up to four eggs per day for four to five weeks. Feeding injury occurs at this time also. When the eggs hatch in seven days, the larvae tunnel into the fruit. The apple drops, and in a few days or a few weeks the larvae leave the fruit to pupate in the soil. If the egg doesn't hatch the fruit doesn't drop but remains scarred.

Identification — Once you've seen curculios or their damage they are difficult to forget. The adult is a snout-nosed black and grey beetle about one-quarter inch long. It has the curious habit of playing possum when disturbed, which makes them easy to identify when knocked out of a tree. Undisturbed, they are active fliers. The identifying injury consists of a crescent-shaped scar in which the egg is laid.

Monitoring — Beginning at bloom and at four to five day intervals check developing fruit from the rows of trees on the southern edge of the orchard, especially if there is an adjacent deciduous woodlot with favorable conditions for overwintering. Gerard Lafleur has found that plum curculio usually migrate north in the spring and south in the autumn. One third of the fruit checked should be in the low inside region of the trees, one third in the low outside region, and one third in the high region of the trees. As soon as the first egg-laying scar is noticed apply a control insecticide. The beetles feed on wild hawthorn trees when they are present before apple trees and it is possible to monitor the insects on this species before they infest the orchard. A hard green apple such as Granny Smith hung in the bushes might attract the egg-laying female and the scars would certainly be easier to see than on pea-sized fruit.

Organic Control — There seem to be no known predators of the beetle in the adult stage and it is only susceptible to full-strength botanical insecticides. Old timers would beat the limbs of the trees with sticks and let the chickens forage on the dropping beetles and egg-infested fruit. Significant reductions in populations would occur if the tiny dropped fruit was cleaned up and poultry will consume some of these drops. The larvae and pupae are intolerant of direct sunlight and only develop in shaded fruit under the trees. The drops should be raked out from under the tree to be exposed to sunlight.

Chemical Control — Imidan full strength. This will probably need to be repeated in seven to ten days. A single spray, delayed five to seven days afer first observation of activity, may suffice for non-commercial orchardists if less than 90 percent control can be tolerated.

Codling Moth

Life Cycle — Moths emerge from cocoons under loose bark scales in late May and June. Males hatch first, followed in about seven days by females. After mating the female moth lays 30 to 40 eggs, first on leaves and twigs, later on fruit. Temperatures above 62 degrees F. in the evening when the moths are most active are necessary to stimulate flights and egg-laying. The eggs hatch in about ten days, depending on the temperature. The worms burrow directly from the blossom end into the core of the fruit to feed and grow. There can be several annual generations depending on the region.

Identification — The moth is grey with brown markings which appear to be bands when the moth is at rest. It is about three-eighths of an inch long when grown. The damage to the fruit is distinctive: the larva usually enters from the blossom end, tunnels directly to the core and leaves a large exit hole. Look for frass at the blossom end.

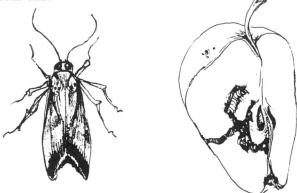

Monitoring — Pheromone traps should be hung in the trees just before bloom. They should not be placed on the orchard periphery. The traps will enable you to decide if controls are necessary, when to apply sprays, and how to use a minimum dosage based on the number of moths captured.

When pheromone traps indicate the presence of the moth, examine the blossom end of the fruit weekly to find entrance holes of larvae. Dispose of these fruit.

Organic Controls — Woodpeckers consume many pupae over-wintering in cocoons. There are other predators, parasites and diseases which keep codling moth in check. Populations are cyclical. Knowing whether the population is increasing or decreasing — keeping accurate records — is important in designing a control program. A ryania application at petal fall has proved effective against codling moth adults. Trichogramma wasps will parasitize codling moth if released three times at two-week intervals beginning at 50 Degree-Days Celsius greater than 11 degrees C. (90 DDF greater than 50 degrees F.). Corrugated cardboard bands (ridges inward) wrapped around the trunks of trees will entice larvae to spin cocoons. These bands can be removed and burned weekly in the summer months. (See September.)

Chemical Controls — Based on one trap per acre, interpret cumulative trap data as follows:

0–60	moths/trap	no control necessary
60–100	moths/trap	Imidan ¼ lb./100 gal.
100–200	moths/trap	Imidan ½ lb./100 gal.
> 200	moths/trap	Imidan 1 lb./100 gal.

Other Mid-season Pests

Borers — There are many species of borers. The flatheaded apple-tree borer is a pest of many trees besides apple. Adult beetles lay eggs on the bark of trunks, usually near the ground, about two to four weeks after petal fall. The larvae tunnel into the bark and feed on the cambium tissue of the tree. The feeding areas appear as sunken depressions from the outside. The grubs can live in the sapwood up to three seasons before emerging as an adult beetle to begin the cycle again. Painting the trunks of trees with a slurry of rotenone and diatomaceous earth will discourage egg laying. Check the trunks often in the summer for entrance holes, usually found with sawdust-like frass below. Probe for the larva with a stiff wire to kill it.

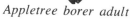

Appletree borer adult

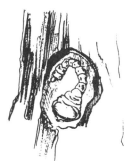

Flatheaded appletree borer larva

Gypsy Moth — In areas where this pest is prevalent, pheromone traps should be hung as soon as the caterpillars appear. Two applications of Bt should control the pest which is a nocturnal feeder. Trichogramma wasps also give some control. Destroying egg masses will certainly help.

Japanese Beetles — These pests appear in late spring, feeding on many plants. They are rarely a problem in orchards, but where they are they are easily controlled with milky spore virus. Some people find that Larkspur planted in the orchard will attract the beetles which die after feeding on the foliage.

Fruit Thinning

Novices often overlook fruit thinning, a simple way to improve the quality of your crop and the health of your trees. Orchardists thin fruit with chemicals that cause a predetermined amount of immature fruit to fall from the tree. On a smaller scale, however, you can thin fruit by hand. The rewards are many: the remaining fruit will be larger and sweeter, harmful insects that damage fruit will have their life cycle interrupted, trees that bear sporadically can be brought to bear every year, and the practice has proven successful in increasing cold hardiness.

Start culling as soon as the fruit starts to swell. Remove all immature fruit that looks stunted, insect damaged or diseased — in other words, all but the best fruit. I begin thinning my apples as soon as the plum curculio appears, usually on a warm day several weeks after petal fall. The curculios leave tiny holes in the pearl-sized fruit. I try to thin all clusters of fruit down to one apple and I like to see the fruits spaced five to six inches along the branch. I'm careful to collect all the fruits I take off.

Fruit should be thinned when it is marble-sized or smaller. The thinned fruit will end up larger and sweeter, and the tree will tend to bear more consistently from year to year.

First Cover Spray

Ten Days After Petal Fall

Insect Pest   **Organic Control**   **Chemical Control**
(Note: control only when monitoring shows evidence)

Insect Pest	Organic Control	Chemical Control
Plum curculio	Repeat Triple-plus	Imidan
Codling moth	Bt with bait or ryania with bait*	Imidan according to trap data
Leafroller	**Bt**	Not necessary
Mites, aphids	Observe buildups	
Gypsy moth	Bt with bait	Imidan
Japanese beetle	Milky spore disease	

Disease
(Note: observe weather to time scab sprays accordingly)

Disease	Organic Control	Chemical Control
Scab	Sulfur Bordeaux — primary spore discharge ending soon	Pre-infection: Polyram Post-infection: see eradicant table (March)
Powdery mildew	Sulfur	
Brown rot (cherries)	Cultivate, remove all mummified fruit; sulfur	
Black knot	Sulfur	Polyram or Phygon
Fire blight	Prune, disinfect tools	Streptomycin — consult extension agent

Fertilizers

All trees	Final foliar feeding spray

* Insect bait is a feeding attractant. See November for pesticide rates.

Summary Sprays

Note: control insects only when traps indicate thresholds are crossed.

Insect Pest	Organic Control	Chemical Control
(Note: control only when monitoring shows evidence)		
Apple maggot	Red ball traps Rotenone Bordeaux spray	Imidan
Codling moth	Bt with bait or ryania with bait*	Imidan according to trap data
Red-banded leaf roller	**Bt**	Imidan according to trap data
Aphids	Control ants Insecticidal soap	Spot application — Malathion
Borers	Insecticidal soap on trunks, probe with wire	Rotenone/diatomaceous earth paste on trunks
Pear psylla	Dust with limestone or diatomaceous earth	Imidan if severe

Disease

Scab ·	When primary discharge is over, protectant sprays are seldom necessary	
Black rot, bitter rot	Sanitation, Bordeaux	Polyram
Sooty blotch, fly speck	These diseases cause minor cosmetic damage, rarely need control	
Brown rot	Sanitation, cultivation Sulfur, especially pre- harvest on peaches	Polyram

* Insect bait is a feeding attractant. See November.

See November for pesticide rates.

66

JULY

- Aphids

- Apple Maggots

- Other Summer Pests

- Leaf Analysis

- Review — Minimizing Pesticides

				1	2	3
Look for leafminers.				Check for borers. Plant a late crop of buckwheat.		
4	**5**	**6**	**7**	**8**	**9**	**10**
Summer prune: apples lightly, peaches up to 50% new growth.				Check for aphids.		
11	**12**	**13**	**14**	**15**	**16**	**17**
Cover cherry trees to keep birds away from fruit.				Remove suckers, watersprouts, allow light into tree to ripen fruit.		
18	**19**	**20**	**21**	**22**	**23**	**24**
Get to know your aphid predators. Clean up all fallen, damaged fruit.				Take leaf samples for analysis — check with extension for best time.		
25	**26**	**27**	**28**	**29**	**30**	**31**
Second generation curculio, codling moth, leafrollers. Cease cultivation to encourage hardening off.				Pre harvest sulfur spray for brown rot peaches.		

67

July

Although I walk through the orchard daily, at least once a week I do a complete inspection of the trees. My standard routine is to start at the base of the trunk, looking for signs of borers. Then I work up and out through the canopy, holding some leaves against the sky so that I can look through them to find leafminer tunnels. At the same time I take notes as to the degree of scab infection or other diseases. Yellowing or discoloration of the leaves is a warning of mineral deficiencies. Finally I check all the insect traps and note the number of bugs trapped for the week.

All this gives me a personal relationship with the trees and the insect populations that are an integral part of the trees. I don't spray according to the calendar but according to need, and I can ascertain the need only with personal interaction with the trees. I am willing to sacrifice a little perfection in the fruit in order to be able to walk through the orchard without the spray suit and respirator. The trees are not covered with poisons and I can climb through the trees without fearing exposure to pesticides.

While climbing through the trees in July I like to do some light summer pruning. I trim out watersprouts which shade the interior of the tree and sap the vigor without directly contributing to the feeding of the developing fruit crop. I don't try to make any major pruning cuts at this time, limiting myself to those obvious non-productive shoots that would have to be taken out next spring anyway. As the watersprouts fall to the ground it is wonderful to see how much more light penetrates to the interior of the tree, giving the fruit and the supportive foliage a much better chance to gain in size, color, and sweetness.

Aphids

There are many species of aphids which live on fruit trees. Some are pests, others are merely transient residents. Except on young trees, a moderate population of aphids can be tolerated without hurting fruit trees. The apple grain aphid, which covers terminal branches in the early part of the season, moves on to other plant species before causing any damage to the apple trees. Aphid control really doesn't need to begin until summer.

Life Cycle — Apple aphid eggs overwinter on the terminal growth and watersprouts of apple trees. Rosy apple aphids overwinter in bark crevices, and woolly apple aphid eggs are laid on the bark of several species. Most of the aphids begin to hatch at the green tip stage of bud development. There can be more than twelve generations each year, with each female giving birth to up to 50 young. Populations build up rapidly, and can seriously stunt terminal growth. This is especially damaging to young trees.

Identification — If the aphid colony has a cottony, woolly white appearance, they are woolly apple aphids. Rosy apple aphids are reddish pink to dark purple in color, and apple aphids are bright green or yellowish with long black honey tubes protruding. A 10x hand lens is essential for identification.

Monitoring — The black eggs of the apple aphid will be apparent on terminal growth in the dormant season. The new growth should be checked weekly during the growing season. At least this pest can't hide from you.

Natural Control — Heavy nitrogen feeding will encourage aphids, so go easy with this nutrient. Planting several plots of buckwheat around the orchard will provide an attractive food source for many beneficial predators and parasites. Ants will actually "farm" aphids, carrying them from place to place to increase their production of honeydew, so controlling ants will help control aphids. This can be accomplished with sticky bands around tree trunks and with a dusting of boron, or solubor spray, on the ground around the trunks. Ants hate boron. Insecticidal soap is somewhat effective against aphids if regularly applied during the growing season. Superior oil in a delayed dormant application is somewhat effective as an ovicide (killing eggs). A combination of several of these methods should give you adequate control without synthetic pesticides.

Chemical Control — Complete control of this pest is seldom necessary; in fact if the aphids are completely eliminated, beneficial predators will be cut off from their livelihood. In severe infestations, especially damaging to young trees, use Malathion sparingly.

Apple Maggots

Life Cycle — Look for maggot flies to emerge from the soil about 30 days after MacIntosh petal fall. Females hatch before males, only a few a day at first, then the hatchings increase in numbers for seven to ten days. After ten days from the first hatching, males and females both hatch in equal numbers for about two weeks. Then the hatching decreases, males being more numerous at this time.

Flies emerge earlier from light sandy soils than from heavy or wet soils, and earlier in warm seasons than in cool years. After emergence the flies mate, and the first eggs are laid seven to ten days after emergence. Early apples, the summer apples, are the first to get the attention of egg laying females.

The female fly finds a suitable apple where she lays her tiny egg inside of the skin of the fruit. Hatching within a week, the larva tunnels through the fruit, completing its development when the apple drops to the ground. The larva burrows into the soil to overwinter in the pupal state.

About one out of ten pupae will not hatch the next spring, remaining dormant for two or more years, making complete control difficult in any one year. Also, wild and neglected apple and hawthorn trees within 300 yards of the orchard are a principal source of infestation.

Identification — The apple maggot fly is slightly smaller than a housefly. The four dark bands on the wings are a sure identification. The female fly has four transverse stripes across the abdomen, the male fly three stripes. A hand lens is helpful in making the distinction. The larva, or worm, in the apple can be distinguished from the codling moth larva by the lack of coloring in the head. The codling moth has a distinct brown head.

Apple Maggot Fly

Monitoring — The flies are attracted upon emergence to foliage on which to feed. A flourescent yellow rectangle, eight by ten inches, covered with a sticky substance such as "tanglefoot" will trap a large number of these early flies seeking food. The flies confuse the rectangle with leaves which appears to them as a super-size leaf. This yellow rectangle will give you an idea of the first hatching date and is easy to use because the flies are easily seen against the bright background. One trap per acre is sufficient for monitoring. Placement of this trap and the following trap is critical: they should be six feet off the ground and should have an area of two feet around the trap clear of foliage.

As soon as flies are identified on the yellow rectangle trap, one should hang the next traps. These are dark red spheres, three inches in diameter. Coated with sticky "tanglefoot" these balls attract the female flies looking for fruit in which to lay their eggs. The large spheres are more attractive than the less developed fruit on the tree. Used at the rate of six per tree, these traps have given 95 percent control of apple maggot damage. The spheres should be checked every five to seven days and the number of catches recorded to give an idea of population levels as the season progresses.

Early maturing varieties are the most suitable place for the traps which should be hung at eye level on the south side of trees in places relatively free of foliage. The new disease resistant variety, Prima, is especially attractive to apple maggot flies (perhaps because they are not covered with fungicides). In general, early ripening varieties are good trees in which to hang the traps.

Apple maggot trap

Organic Controls — There are no effective predators of the maggot fly so the best natural control consists of a combination of sanitation and trapping, continued for several years. Removing wild trees infested with maggots near the orchard will lesson the influx of flies into the orchard. Wild hawthorn is another host of the apple maggot, and these should be eliminated up to a three quarter mile radius.

Apple maggot flies are susceptible to pyrethrum, rotenone, and diatomaceous earth. Susan Opp at the University of Massachusetts has recently discovered that Bordeaux spray (copper sulfate and lime) will effectively deter female apple maggot flies from laying eggs in fruit. This fungicide could be used to control both summer diseases and maggot damage. However Bordeaux spray is likely to cause phytotoxicity and russetting. See March.

Chemical Control — Use Imidan when traps indicate emergence. Consider using perimeter sprays.

Other Summer Pests

Fall Webworm — These caterpillars form webs on the ends of branches similar to tent caterpillar tents. The caterpillar itself is much hairier and doesn't emerge until summer, distinguishing it from the spring-hatching tent caterpillar. There are several generations. Webworms can be manually removed from the trees or sprayed with several doses of Bt.

Buffalo Treehopper — Damage from these hoppers is from the punctures made in the bark when the adult females lay eggs. The puncture leaves a crescent shaped scar, and the egg overwinters under the bark. In severe infestations trees are stunted, scaly and cracked. The alternate hosts of this pest include clovers and other legumes which should not be planted where populations are known to exist. Superior oil sprays which drench the trunks give some control of the dormant eggs.

Leaf Analysis

The nutrients in the soil may or may not be available to the trees depending on many factors and variables in the root/soil interface. The best way to be certain of the nutrient needs of trees is through a leaf analysis. This is a sophisticated analysis in which the mineral levels of a leaf sample are compared against a statistical optimum.

Consult with your county extension agent for information on how leaf samples are taken in your area. Most states will collect samples at a specific time of year, usually July, and charge a minimal fee for the laboratory analysis. Some extension services may recommend private laboratories that do analysis. Typically, one collects 100 leaves from the variety being tested, sending them to the lab in a perforated plastic bag. Make arrangements for testing in the spring.

What you will receive from the laboratory is a sheet comparing nutrient levels in your trees to what they should be. For example, the test might show that the level of boron in your trees is 40 parts per million (ppm). Compare this to the norm which is usually given in a range, such as 35 ppm to 50 ppm. Your sample of 40 ppm falls in the lower end of the range indicating that you should add some boron to the tree's diet. These analyses save a lot of money in specifically tailoring your fertilizer program to the needs of your trees.

Review — Minimizing Pesticides

A program to minimize damage to beneficial insects by decreasing pesticide use should include the following tactics:

- Sanitation — cleaning up the orchard and its surroundings is the single most important factor in reducing pest populations.
- Timing — monitoring populations and weather conditions.
- Early knockdown — lowering populations of pests at the beginning of the increase to give predators a chance to control and reduce secondary hatchings.
- Minimum dosages — and avoiding over-spraying. For some insects, such as codling moth, one quarter stength will give adequate control where populations (as determined by trapping) are moderate. Other insects, such as plum curculio, may need full dosages to give effective control.
- Alternate side spraying — spraying one side of the tree one week and the other side the next week. This saves up to 50 percent of insecticides. Mobile insects, such as codling moths and apple maggots, will contact the poison in their travels through the trees. This technique is less effective against non-mobile insects such as mites and aphids. However, predators will be encouraged by this method of spraying and mites and aphids should be controlled naturally.

For example, apple maggot populations may be high enough to warrant two insecticide applications. By spraying one half of each tree one week, and the other half the next week, two sprays will have been accomplished with the same amount of pesticide as one normal application.

Alternate side spraying should be used cautiously if diseases are a problem. Thorough coverage of the trees with a fungicide is important for disease control. However, alternate side spraying has proven to be highly effective for disease control if spray penetration is good and if spray intervals are frequent (seven to ten days).

- Perimeter spraying — using insecticides only on the perimeter of the orchard to control migrating insects as they move into the orchard. This has shown some effectiveness against curculio, maggot and codling moth.

AUGUST

- Special Needs of Pears, Peaches, Plums and Cherries

- Special Care for Young Trees

- Cleaning Insect Traps

- The Bio-dynamic Approach to Orchards

				1	2	3
				Start summer bud grafting.		
4	5	6	7	8	9	10
Check for borers, especially peaches.				Remove dropped peaches weekly to discourage brown rot.		
11	12	13	14	15	16	17
Start to harvest peaches when background color yellows.				Water new trees deeply.		
			Watch for secondary scab infections.			
18	19	20	21	22	23	24
Clean insect traps in warm weather - the job gets more difficult with time.				Pick fruit in cool weather, chill immediately for storage.		
25	26	27	28	29	30	31
Keep all windfalls cleaned up.				Turn mulch.		
				Keep grass mowed close for a cleaner harvest.		

August

During the dry months I pay special attention to the mulch in the orchard, keeping it fluffed up and thick to preserve the precious moisture necessary for the swelling fruit. Several years of drought conditions in which the young trees under mulch were the only ones to thrive convinced me that I'd rather mulch than irrigate. The combination of keeping the grass between rows mowed close and the mulch in the rows thick but loose has proven to me that irrigation is not necessary in my climate.

One thing that is necessary in any climate is daily patrolling for dropped fruit. I carry a grainbag with me and scoop up drops whenever I can. Sometimes I cut a fallen fruit open and find a developing larva inside which would have continued to haunt me in succeeding generations if I hadn't interrupted its life cycle at this vulnerable stage.

Sometimes I'll find an apple with a codling moth entrance tunnel in the blossom end and no exit hole through the side of the fruit. This too goes into the sack because I know that there is a little worm inside. While I lug this bag around I console myself with the thought that every larva I remove now will mean hundreds less the next year. I know there will still be plenty but if I want to spray less I have to clean up. Always.

Late summer walks through the trees give me an opportunity to mentally size up the crop and prepare for the hectic picking season to come. I note which trees are bearing well and which are not. I inspect the fruit for damage from insects and disease, mentally tallying up the percentage of the crop that will go into cider. It's the wrong time of the year to prune, it's too late to do much about insects, so the orchard walks take on a more relaxed and reflective nature. There is even time to skip down to the pond for a swim.

Special Needs of Pears, Peaches, Plums, and Cherries

The cultural information is similar for all tree crops, most certainly the emphasis on sanitation and monitoring. Serious growers of fruits will want to study their particular crop in more depth. The following is meant only as an overview. Your local growers are the best source of information.

Pears — Pears are susceptible to most of the pests which bother apples. Controls are basically the same. Pears are very prone to fire blight infections so a strong effort must be made to control sucking insects which spread the bacteria. These insects include aphids, mites, and the pear psylla.

Pear psylla, yellow to orange in color, are similar in size to large winged aphids. The orange eggs appear on twigs and at the base of buds before bloom. Often the insect is detected only later in the season when a sooty mold fungus becomes apparent on leaves and fruit. This fungus grows in the honeydew excreted by the psylla. Leaves and fruit blackened with severe sooty mold drop early.

Look for pear psylla on the highest shoots of new growth. Control early in the season with a split spray of dormant oil (one half concentration at green tip and another at one half inch green). Psylla can be controlled later in the season with a dusting of limestone or diatomaceous earth. Insecticidal soap has shown some effectiveness. Use Imidan only in extreme situations.

Pear slugs are the larvae of a sawfly. They appear on the leaves in early summer as small, olive-green, slimy slugs and quickly begin to skeletonize the leaves. Wood ashes or rotenone dusted on them are very effective controls.

Cultural needs of pears are similar to apples. Be very careful not to apply too much nitrogen to pears as this tends to increase succulent growth which is highly susceptible to sucking insects and thus fire blight. It is better to hold back on nitrogen, especially raw manures, unless a definite need is established by leaf analysis, soil analysis, or observation.

Peaches — Peach trees are heavy feeders. To insure good cropping and resistance to disease and insects, attention must be paid to fertilization. Peaches need a good supply of potassium, as long as it is balanced with adequate nitrogen. Calcium is also very important. A consistently cared for hay mulch will supply ample potassium, but under a mulch calcium and magnesium will probably have to be added. Keep up to date with soil testing and leaf analysis.

Thinning is very important for peaches. They tend to over-set fruit, resulting in heavy crops of low quality. It is important to thin early, before the fruit is walnut-sized. Space the fruits six inches apart along the branches. Thinning can be done by hand or, as in some commercial orchards, by whacking the branches with a four foot pole with an eighteen-inch rubber hose on the end. Some hand thinning will be necessary in any case.

Peach tree borers are a major problem in some areas. Adult female moths emerge in early summer and lay eggs on or near tree trunks. The worms hatch in ten days, boring into the bark just below the soil surface. Damage due to girdling can be devastating. A pheromone mating disruptive has proven to be an effective control of peach tree borer. See September.

Brown rot of peaches is a fungus disease compounded by injury caused by insects. The most effective control is a strict sanitation program, cleaning up all dropped, diseased or mummified fruit before the spores have a chance to spread. Use a micro-fine sulfur spray three to four weeks before harvest.

Plums, and Cherries — Prunus Species — Plums and cherries can suffer from many of the pests of apples, especially maggot flies and plum curculio. Control is the same as for apples, with the emphasis on sanitation.

Oriental fruit moth is a pest of prunus species. Shortly after bloom, check new shoots for wilting of the terminal growth. Larvae are one half inch long, pink, and very active when disturbed. Later generations enter the fruit and spoil it from within. Bt will control the larvae, and should be applied shortly after bloom. Shallow cultivation before bloom will help destroy overwintering pupae.

Cherry fruit fly is very similar to the apple maggot fly and monitoring and control is virtually the same.

Black knot fungus is a serious problem for prunus species. Black, hard, lumpy swellings are scattered throughout limbs and twigs. Often these are seen in hedgerows on wild cherries and plums. The disease is difficult to control once established in the orchard. Remove wild hosts, prune and burn infected branches regularly. Be sure to prune four to five inches below the visible infection, and sterilize pruners between cuts with a 1:10 bleach solution.

Special Care for Young Trees

The first years of a tree's growth are critical. You can't plant a new tree and neglect it until it starts to bear fruit. Soil fertility, pruning, and pest management go hand in hand in the development of a healthy productive tree. Modern pruning techniques place much emphasis on the first five years of the tree's growth, but in this non-bearing period many growers don't take the time to protect their plantings from pests and maintain a fertilization program.

Mature trees can better afford a lapse in management than new plantings. In the established orchard, especially where pest management techniques have been used, insect populations are relatively stable and disease will rarely threaten to kill the trees. Young orchards are susceptible to sudden swings in insect balances because pests and predators have not attained a balance. Diseases can seriously damage young trees. This I found out after losing half of my initial planting to winterkill after a summer of severe scab weakened the trees.

Young trees are easy to monitor for insects because of their size. Look at the terminal growth for aphids and check weekly for leafrollers. It is easy to hand pick insects while the trees are small, but when infestations are high it is better to use insecticides than to take a chance with pest damage. I stop spraying for aphids in July, because it has been shown that some aphid activity on the terminals will actually help harden off the new growth for winter.

Disease control on young trees should be diligent. New growth is very prone to fungus infections, especially scab. These diseases, if left uncontrolled, can infect woody tissue as well as foliage, seriously stunting the tree growth. Weakened by disease, trees are open to attack by insects and prone to winter damage. White latex paint on the south and west sides of the tender trunks will help prevent winter bark splitting and will also help deter the buffalo treehopper.

Pay attention to the tree trunk — soil line area. Don't let weeds grow up around the base of the trunk giving shelter to borers and mice. Keep this area clear and check often in the summer for borers. Mulch or shallow cultivation will help young trees get a good start. Make sure that each tree has a wire mesh mouse guard before winter.

Cleaning Insect Traps

Many insect traps are designed to be disposable, especially the pheromone traps. Newer ones have removable sections that are replaced so that the entire trap doesn't need to be thrown away, just the tanglefoot-coated part. The red balls that are used to trap apple maggots need to be cleaned and stored carefully to be ready for the next season. It is best to do this chore before the weather turns cool and the tanglefoot gets hardened. Many times I've seen these traps hanging in the trees all winter, getting steadily more difficult to clean.

I use a two pound coffee can with turpentine to clean the wooden balls. If the tanglefoot is really hardened on, I put the can full of turpentine into a pail of very hot water to warm up the solvent first. With a little soaking and a good scrubbing with an old dishwashing brush, the tanglefoot comes off neatly.

I hang the clean traps from a beam in the barn. Over the winter the turpentine smell will evaporate. I don't know if the solvent odor would keep maggot flies away but I don't want to take the chance. It's better to give the traps a good airing and to have them ready to go into the trees when the time is right.

The Bio-dynamic Approach to Orchards

The Bio-dynamic school of agriculture evolved from eight lectures given to farmers by Rudolf Steiner in 1924. Steiner was the founder of the spiritual science of Anthroposophy. This school of thought has been influential in many disciplines, especially education, medicine and architecture. One of the aims of Anthroposophy is "to create an awareness in the minds of men that behind the physical phenomena of nature an external spirituality comes to expression." Also, "to connect the spiritual in the human being with this spiritual in the world."

Bio-dynamics is both a practical, scientific, approach to agriculture and a wholistic world view. This discipline regards the earth as a living organism and the farm as a self-contained individuality. The theories of Bio-dynamics, based on this ecological viewpoint, attempt to bring into balance the processes which create and maintain life. In this concept plant growth develops under the influence of cosmic and terrestrial polarities. In practice this involves enlivening soil life activity by composting organic materials with the aid of specific preparations and balancing earthly (humid, mineral, vegetative) and atmospheric (dry, light, fruiting) forces with special sprays.

Given as a central imagination in the agricultural course is the image of the farm viewed as an organism that is naturally productive when brought into a self-contained and individual state of dynamic balance. The ruminating animal especially the cow forms the central focus for the streaming in and out of substances and forces on the farm. All other animals, crops and field management complete this picture through their unique contribution to the being of the farm as a whole.

In his lectures Steiner explained the idea that "the tree is really earth grown up like a hillock" and that the branches grow out of the cambium that acts as a "matted root layer" in the same way as herbaceous annuals grow from the soil. He also described the intimate relation of trees to the insect and bird kingdoms. The bees in particular bring special substances in highly dilute amounts into the atmosphere of the farm. Substances like Apis, the stinging substance of the bees, are highly valued in homeopathic medicine for their healing and regulating properties. It is these references and this type of thinking that create the basis for Bio-dynamic work on the farm and in the orchard.

The late Peter Escher, a Bio-dynamic orchard consultant, developed a tree paste that is applied to tree bark enlivening the cambium, healing wounds, and smothering pests. This paste is composed of a fine clay like bentonite, fresh cow manure, and a Bio-dynamic preparation. The tree paste is often used in place of a dormant oil spray as the clay can (like oil) provide a water and air impermeable layer on branches and bark. Rotenone, pyrethrum, and ryania can also be mixed in when a known insect infestation exists. The healing of this paste, compared with asphalt-based dressings, is remarkable. The use of a Bio-dynamically prepared compost around the expanding drip-line root zones is essential in Bio-dynamic orchards, as is the use of the two special sprays, the "Horn Manure" to stimulate the life of the soil and the "Horn Silica" to enhance the structure and ripening in leaves and fruit. European trials have shown that Bio-dynamic management, including the use of proper fertilizers (especially cow-manure-based compost fortified with bone meal), greatly reduces pest and disease problems.

Bio-dynamic orchardists in the northeast must still make use of sulfur as a fungicide especially during primary infection stages of apple scab. During later sprays they substitute a preventative spray based on equisetum arvense (the horsetail plant). This plant is primarily composed of silica which Bio-dynamic practitioners regard as an anti-fungal element. The silica principle is also utilized in sprays of Bio-dynamically prepared quartz powder. Water glass (sodium silicate) is sometimes used. Part of the rigid Bio-dynamic sanitation practices include the picking up of all dropped fruit and the composting or spraying of old leaves to reduce disease spore loads.

Alice Bennett-Groh, a leading Bio-dynamic orchardist, has described orcharding as "gardening higher in the atmosphere." It is this type of conceptualization that forms the core of the Bio-dynamic approach.

SEPTEMBER

- Soil, Site and Tree Health
- Planting Preparation
- Promising Developments. . .
- Tuning In to Nature

				1	2	3
			Remove dropped fruit twice weekly.		Pick pears slightly green.	
4	**5**	**6**	**7**	**8**	**9**	**10**
	Continue borer control, especially in the south.			Buffalo treehoppers lay eggs in bark — check for crescent shaped scars.		
11	**12**	**13**	**14**	**15**	**16**	**17**
	Test soil for nematodes.			Cardboard bands trap second generation codling moths.		
18	**19**	**20**	**21**	**22**	**23**	**24**
	Order next year's nursery stock now — get best selection.			Check old trees and wild trees for desirable varieties.		
25	**26**	**27**	**28**	**29**	**30**	
	Pre-harvest mowing is important.			Fall preparation for spring planting.		

September

I keep the orchards mowed closely in September, in anticipation of the harvest and to make it easier to pick up windfalls. Before mowing, I check carefully between the rows for any fruit that would be cut up by the mower. Some of the fallen fruit is good for sauce, some is fine for cider. What is not suitable for cooking or for squeezing is fed to the animals.

Mowing the orchard can be a challenge. I used to use a seven foot cutter bar until I clipped a young tree trying to mow too closely. Even with a lawn mower or a bush hog, one has to be aware of damaging trees, or hitting low branches, rocks and ruts. When the noisy chore is done, I can look back with satisfaction at the groomed order of the trees loaded down with fruit.

This is a good time to mark out the new block of trees that have been ordered for next year. With a tape measure, some twine and some stakes I mark a grid on the newly harrowed section on the other side of the lane. I will be planting semi-dwarf trees here where the soil is deep so I space them fifteen feet apart in each row, leaving eighteen feet between rows. On poorer soils I would rather plant standard trees with vigorous rootstocks. Standard trees are definitely more forgiving of part-time orchardists.

It is a pleasure to dig holes in September instead of during the mud season of spring. I take care to dig large holes, at least a meter in diameter. The lateral roots of fruit trees grow very quickly and I like to give them plenty of room. I mix some rock powders in with the topsoil, piling it on the uphill side of the hole. Then I cover the site with a broken bale of hay before going on to the next hole. Come spring, it will be easy to plant the new nursery stock and the soil will be well blended by frost.

Walking back through the fruit laden trees something catches my eye, and looking closer, I find an apple with a codling moth hole. Too late to catch the worm, I pick the spoiled fruit anyway and put it in the box of cider apples at the end of the row. Somewhere, the larva that spoiled the fruit has spun a cocoon and will spend the next eight months slowly becoming a moth. Many of the insect pests of the orchard are dormant now, or soon to be dormant. I try to interrupt the endless life cycles by disposing of wormy fruit, but some insects always get through the net.

Soil, Site, and Tree Health

A tree that is growing on poor soil or in a poor location will never be as healthy or as productive as a tree that is located where it has fertile soil and a favorable location. Those who plant in poor locations are doing themselves a disservice. Those who have existing trees in the wrong spot are fighting a long, uphill battle. Drainage is the key, both in the soil and in air circulation. Fruit trees simply cannot tolerate poor drainage.

The best soils are deep, light in texture and well drained without being droughty. Well drained soils can always be improved with green manures, compost and other soil building practices. Clay soils and soils susceptible to waterlogging should be ruled out for fruit trees.

Sometimes fruit trees can be established on poor soils with a combination of chisel plowing, drain tile and proper rootstock selection. Because soils and rootstock viability vary so much from area to area, your local extension office can give you current recommendations. If you have marginal soil you might want to experiment with several rootstocks.

Rapid drying of foliage is essential to minimize disease infections, and air circulation is the key to rapid foliage drying. The maxim "always plant on a slope" is especially true for those wishing to reduce fungicide sprays. Orchards should be located on high ground where there is no interference with natural airflow. The compass orientation of the slope is not as important as the amount of air circulation on the slope. In northern latitudes, northern slopes will minimize winter damage and delay blossoming, possibly preventing frost damage.

Planting Preparation

Planting new trees can be a yearly program — whether those trees are new disease resistant varieties or old standard varieties. Seldom does one plant the first tree as well as later ones. Every existing condition is different, but several common factors are important to emphasize:

• Use existing topsoil and subsoil whenever possible. I mix sand or gravel in with subsoil as needed for drainage. Then I soak this base thoroughly — it's best to let it set all winter. If the base is not compacted the tree might settle, forming a "basin." The object is to have water drain away from the trunk.

- Remember that the feeding zone of roots is shallow — especially in northern climates with cold soils. Do not add compost or manure below the depth of the existing organic top soil. Humus added below this depth has the potential of rotting and putrefying.

- Blend soil amendments with existing loam well. Add limestone to bring pH to 6.5 for apples, 6.0 for plums, peaches and cherries.

- After the tree has been planted and the soil firmed around the roots with the fingers, DO NOT pack the soil any more with the feet. Instead, water thoroughly and slowly until the hole is filled with water. Then gently agitate the tree, or probe with a stick to "burp" any air pockets.

- If possible, stake the tree for the first season. At the very least, firm and mound soil around the trunk/soil interface. This interface is the site of many problems with young trees. Pay attention to it.

- Water well and consistently throughout the season. Mulch is very helpful with young trees.

Mulch is most effective if it is turned often, and moved away from the tree in the autumn.

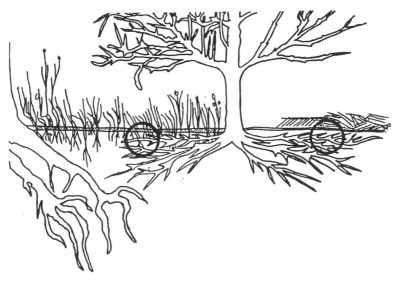

The root zone of fruit trees is very susceptible to competition from other trees, weeds and brambles. Eighty percent of the feeding roots are within the top eight inches of soil. Shallow cultivation and a well-kept mulch are the first steps toward restoration of older trees.

Roots from competing plants, impermeable layers of thatch, shallow soils and drainage problems limit healthy tree growth.

Feeding roots thrive in well aerated soil with high humus content. This is best attained by shallow cultivation and mulch.

Promising Developments. . .

Many books and articles on ecological pest control, including this one, include a hopeful note that research in progress may provide a breakthrough for those seeking alternatives to pesticides. These "promising developments" have many similarities: positive indications of effectiveness, and lack of money for research, development, and the incredibly expensive regulatory process. Often new methods of pest control turn out to be too expensive for large scale applications.

A number of alternative pest programs have been tested, including: male insect sterilization; juvenile hormones; viral and other diseases; and the introduction of predator and parasite species.

These control methods, usually developed by university scientists, have not become easily available to growers. The complex nature (compared to "simple" pesticides), decreasing government funding for this type of research, and the lack of commercial incentive have kept these methods "off the shelf."

For example, codling moth granulosis virus (CMGV) is a viral disease that affects lepidoptera larvae. It was first discovered in 1963 and successfully tested in western orchards in 1981 to 1982. Yet it is not on the market because government regulatory agencies (that were originally intended to reduce pesticide dangers) have become a roadblock to alternative pest control products. The other reason why you can't buy products like this from orchard suppliers is because they are more expensive to produce and market than conventional insecticides.

Less developed but possibly of great importance, has been the research on several beneficial fungi. Fungi antagonistic to apple scab have been effectively tested in Wisconsin and a fungus that attacks the plum curculio is under commercial development in Ohio. Also, Safers Agro Chem who developed insecticidal soaps, are testing fungicidal soaps.

These "promising developments" and many others will not be available to orchardists unless there is a demand by consumers for organically grown fruit, and subsequent demand for orchardists to use more expensive, sophisticated and ecologically sound controls.

Many orchardists have worked out their own pest control programs. A.P. Thompson of Virginia vacuums up fallen apple leaves to reduce scab spore loads. Alvin Filsinger of Ontario has been using a series of "black lights" to control codling moth in his orchards. Peter

Escher achieved some control of fungus diseases with sprays of water glass (sodium silicate). Charles Young of Connecticut has been using Shaklee "Basic G" to battle apple scab. Some people have experimented with urine, at one fourth dilution to control scab. Others are using "bug juice" — solutions containing blended insects (and perhaps diseases) to discourage pests.

While none of these "promising developments" have been overwhelmingly successful they illustrate the need for scientific development of ecologically acceptable methods. Meanwhile, the burden of experimentation will fall upon small growers and researchers daring enough to try different approaches.

Tuning In To Nature

"Tuning in to Nature — Solar Energy, Infrared Radiation and the Insect Communication System" is the full title of a book by Dr. Philip Callahan. Dr. Callahan is a research scientist with the U.S.D.A. in Gainsville, Florida. This book is just one of a series of his explanations of the insect world and low-level energy phenomena. Callahan explains in great detail how the world is perceived by insects, and shows that insect antennae are energy receptors of incredible sensitivity. Callahan reveals that sex pheromones are chemicals released by females to attract males not by scent but by narrow based infrared signals.

Pheromones are just one of many examples of the electromagnetic communication world of insects. Callahan's theories may even indicate that insects attack unhealthy plants because the "unbalanced" plants give off a frequency that insects tune into. These theories may lead to new methods of insect control.

Callahan imagines that "The farmer, instead of going to a store to buy a bag of insecticide will buy, or lease, a little microminiature transmitter that either attracts the insect species attacking his crop or conversely, beats against the insect pheromone frequency and jams it so that mating does not take place. . .There is one final practical advantage to such an insect control device in addition to its ability to attract only the selected species to which it is tuned: it can be turned off when not in use. That is precisely what is wrong with insecticides — they cannot be turned off."

An aspect of this idea has been put into practice with the use of pheromone mating disruptives. These pheromones are sprayed in the orchard and have been commercially successful for control of peach tree borers and in boll weevils. A mating disruptive for codling moth has shown 90 percent control in the Pacific northwest.

One other aspect of Callahan's work is the investigation of low level energy receptors. Callahan believes that there are many agricultural applications for attracting low level energy to fields and orchards. This idea is now being marketed by a few "radionics" companies in North America. Selling antennae shaped units with names like "Towers of Power" and "The Cosmic Pipeline" these entrepreneurs are claiming that their units will improve quality and yields on farms.

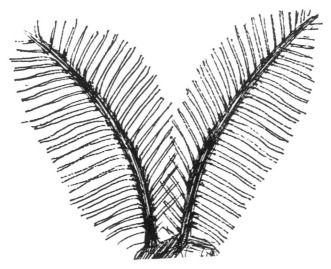

The structure of insect antennae, such as these highly magnified moth antennae, serve as a model for complex radio antennae designed to tune in to specific frequencies.

OCTOBER

- Harvest and Storage

- Identifying Pests From Fruit Scars

- Marketing Certified Organic Fruit

- Old Varieties

				1	2	3
				Take soil samples for testing.		
4	5	6	7	8	9	10
Examine fruit at harvest to identify and quantify damage from pests.						
11	12	13	14	15	16	17
Turn mulch to discourage mice. Mark wild trees you want to take scions from next winter.				Clean up drops daily.		
18	19	20	21	22	23	24
Record all harvest dates. Winterize sprayers.				Let cider apples ripen before pressing.		
25	26	27	28	29	30	31
Rake up and burn leaves if practical. Check mouse guards.				Apples bloom in Australia.		

October

There are many wild and abandoned orchards that I prowl in the fall. I scavenge the old varieties in search of favorites. Some of them have no names. There is a dark beauty on the ridge, a small apple with a taste that is still refreshing in April. The wizened old tree has withstood years of exposure to bitter cold and harsh wind. With no attention, this tree produces a bumper crop of beautiful fruit. The owner hasn't time to care for the trees so he lets me pick the apples for my cellar.

Some of the old orchards are long overgrown and the brambles have taken over. I scrape and crawl through the burdock and black-berry bushes to pick a few special fruits. I say to myself that I'll never let my orchard get this way, at the same time knowing that the orchard will be there long after I'm taking care of it. I wonder who, fifty years from now, will be picking fruit from the trees I planted.

Some of the wild trees I visit yield perfect fruit with no care at all, and these are the ones I will mark to take scions from for grafting next spring. There is a russet apple at the neighbor's farm that makes a delicious cider. In trade for a few gallons of cider he lets me harvest the fruit. I grafted a dozen trees with scions from his tree so that this variety will be available for others.

Walking down the rows of my orchard again, I cut into a few apples, noting the development of the seeds. I compare this year's observations of weather and degree days with the records of previous years, deciding upon an optimum harvest date. I want the fruit that goes into storage to be harvested a little early so that it will taste fresh in March. My goal is to store five bushels of fancy fruit, to put up fifty gallons of cider, and to sell the rest of the crop. Almost half of my harvest goes into cider, for which there is a steady demand. Good cider captures a wonderful essence of the fruit and there are many combinations of varieties that produce different tastes. As I grade out fruit that is whole and of keeping quality, I am thankful for having taken precautions during the year to control damaging insects and disease in my orchard. Nevertheless, I gladly accept a percentage of juice-quality fruit as long as I don't have to spray pesticides every week.

There is a satisfying feeling in picking my own trees clean. It seems as if the trees breath a sigh of relief as the branches, relieved of their burden, lighten and arch upward again. As the colorful fruit fills the boxes, the culmination of the year's effort is measured in bushels and the balance sheet is drawn as to whether it was a healthy and profitable year.

Harvest and Storage

It is important to harvest fruit at the right stage of maturity. Your location, the variety, time of bloom, and summer conditions will determine what your harvest date will be. Decide on a harvest date for each variety in your orchard and plan for this to be the mid-point of harvest for storage fruit, or the starting date for fresh fruit. Generally, storage fruit should be harvested a week or two before maximum ripeness. Dr. Warren Stiles of Cornell has said that "fruit maturity at time of harvest is perhaps more important than any other factor in determining fruit quality following storage." It is important to remove the field heat of fruits as quickly as possible and harvest the fruit without bruising.

At harvest, identify which trees are bearing well and which are not. Keep a log of the harvest from each tree or each part of the orchard. Note the healthy trees and the deficient ones, and compare previous year's records. Select at least a hundred fruit at random and inspect them carefully for damage. Figure out the percentage for each pest, then decide if more or less controls are needed for the following year. Only you can decide whether you can tolerate 5 percent or 50 percent damaged fruit. Admittedly there are plenty of other things to do at harvest time, but the orchard calendar is always full, and taking time now to take a few notes will save time and money in the next growing season.

Storage — Home orchardists need only a cold cellar to store fruit for the winter. However, fruit to be stored should be free of any injuries that puncture the skin. It is critical to cool the fruit to be stored as quickly as possible after harvest. Apples cooled to 36 degrees in six weeks keep until December 20th. Apples cooled to 36 degrees in seven days keep until January 15th. Apples cooled to 32 degrees in seven days keep until April 15th. For each week of delay in cooling deduct a month from storage life.

Some storage problems commonly encountered are shriveling and fruit rots. Shriveling is a result of low humidity in the storage atmosphere. Fruit harvested when immature loses moisture more rapidly than fully mature fruit. Storage in ventilated polyethylene bags helps reduce shriveling. Storage rot is a catch-all term for fungus decay. In apples this is primarily a blue mold. Riper fruits decay faster, and skin breaks are frequently the entry point of fungus. Low storage temperature retards decay, but most important is storage room sanitation.

Identifying Pests From Fruit Scars

Many insects are difficult to find in the orchard, especially for people who are just learning to monitor pests and don't know what to look for. With traps, it is easy to lure some insects for positive identification. However, there aren't traps for all insects.

All pests leave scars on the fruit and learning to identify which insect left what scar is important, not only in identifying potential problems, but also in assessing if your control measures are working. Although this identification is "after the fact," it is often the only way that novices can learn what pests they are dealing with.

The first time to examine fruit is during the "June drop " when trees naturally shed a percentage of immature fruit. At this time it is possible to identify the feeding and egg-laying scars of plum curculio. Over 90 percent of the fruit in which curculio eggs were laid drop to the ground at this time. Also, green fruitworm damage is evident at this time. The fruitworms eat large sections from the small, marble-sized fruit.

Later in the season, examination of the swelling fruit may reveal the curving, russetted scars of European apple sawfly. Deep dimples in the fruit can be the result of egg-laying or feeding by several species of plant bugs, and differentiation is difficult. Codling moth damage begins to show up in the summer. Many times these apples will drop.

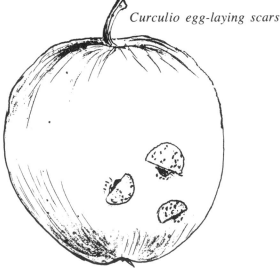

Curculio egg-laying scars

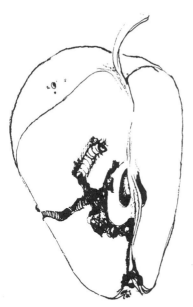

Codling moth larva

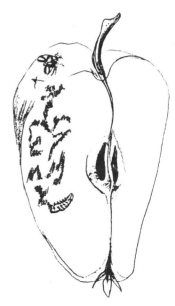

Apple maggot fly and "railroad worm" larva

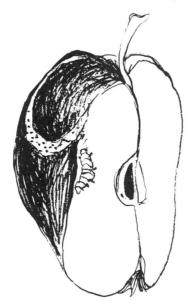

European apple sawfly scar and larva

Apple maggot spend more time in the fruit than codling moth, and it is important to learn to identify the difference between these two worms if one is going to control them. The maggot burrows through the fruit leaving a system of thin tunnels that turn brown from oxidation. The meandering tunnels gave it the nickname of "railroad worm." Usually this is the worm that is found in the fruit at harvest.

Identification of insect damage will help you prepare for the next year. You can also keep track of which ones are causing enough damage to warrant control.

Marketing Certified Organic Fruit

There is a large demand for "organically grown" fruit. In the past few years there has been a major shift in the market place. Consumers are demanding nutritious and residue-free food. Nutrition has replaced price as the main concern of shoppers. Market surveys also report this concern includes a widespread dislike of chemical residues or additives of any kind.

Organic food wholesalers and processors are searching for orchardists who can grow commercial volumes of "organic" fruit. In the past the designation of fruit as "organic" was a matter of trust between the grower and consumer. As the "organic" market has expanded a more formal certification procedure has emerged. Certification organizations can be managed by agricultural associations as a service to their members, by businesses as an in-house quality control, or by the growers themselves.

The certification process is based on a set of standards or rules that define what materials or practices can be classified as "organic." Verification of these standards usually includes an affadavit, a questionnaire, independent field inspections and laboratory analysis. There is a good deal of controversy about the scientific basis for making decisions on what can be labelled "organic." Areas of contention include manufactured fertilizers such as urea, calcium nitrate, potassium nitrate and potassium sulfate, processed micronutrients such as chelated minerals or solubor, pesticides such as copper formulations and numerous synergists and stabilizers in "natural" pesticides.

It is the role of certification organizations to develop more accurate criteria based on the environmental impact of products and practices, in order to establish realistic standards and procedures.

The organic schedules mentioned in this almanac should be acceptable to most certification programs but it is essential that the grower contact a certification organization long before he intends to market organic fruit. It normally takes a year of involvement with a group before arrangements are made to certify a crop. Each organization has distinctive standards, time requirements required for transition from chemical to organic management, and soil and residue testing requirements.

Record-keeping is essential for certification. All soil and leaf analysis, fertilizer applications, spray schedules, block by block yields, and financial transactions involving the sale of organic products must be clearly recorded. This necessary bureaucracy will in return aid the grower in his/her own planning and management.

The creation of a credible "organic" product in the marketplace will take a combined effort of growers, wholesalers and retailers. As consumer confidence builds and marketplace demand grows the difficult task of organic orchard management will pay off.

BUY

THE ORGANIC FOODS PRODUCTION ASSOCIATION OF NORTH AMERICA (OFPANA)

Old Varieties

Many old varieties of fruit trees are living examples of natural resistance to insects and diseases. Often these old varieties were grown for specifically that reason, but fell out of favor as pesticides made possible newer, more tender varieties. Certainly the old Wealthy apples, or the russet varieties were successful in their day because they were relatively unaffected by insects and disease. In every region of North America there are local varieties that show natural resistance. Usually there are some common characteristics such as late ripening and thick skin. Although these varieties may never make it to the commercial orchard, they belong in the home orchard.

There are many reasons for the preservation of old varieties. One is simply the preservation of the genetic diversity which is rapidly being lost. Also, regional peculiarities may produce especially adapted varieties. Many of the best known cultivars were discovered as seedling fruit from unknown parentage. A careful canvassing of your locality will probably turn up more than one unnamed but worthy variety that should be preserved.

My favorite local variety is the Black Oxford, not mentioned in any text that I have found. The trees are hardy, prolific, and annual bearing if thinned. The fruit is dark red, almost black in color. It is somewhat thick-skinned but very juicy, the taste is wonderful, and it keeps well into April in cold storage. Best of all, it seems to be unaffected by insects or disease.

There is no reason why homeowners need to grow the standard supermarket varieties of fruit when there are so many interesting old varieties that taste wonderful and are resistant to pests. Make your home orchard a special one and plant some different varieties. Be sure to plant some of the new disease immune varieties, but don't overlook the diversity available in the old varieties.

NOVEMBER

- Using Pesticides Safely

- Bacillus Thuringiensis — A Microbial Insecticide

- Botanical Insecticides

- Diatomaceous Earth

- Enzyme Ticket Pesticide Detectors

- Insecticide Rates

- Fungicide Rates

- Synthetic Chemical Pesticides

				1	2	3
				Install and check mouse guards.		
4	**5**	**6**	**7**	**8**	**9**	**10**
	Mow orchard before snowfall.			Paint south side of trees white to prevent winter sunscald. Use white interior latex.		
11	**12**	**13**	**14**	**15**	**16**	**17**
Rake and burn leaves.			Winterize equipment, drain and lubricate pumps.			
		Check deer fence or repellents.				
18	**19**	**20**	**21**	**22**	**23**	**24**
Cultivate around cherries, plums, peaches to discourage brown rot.				Turn all mulches and rake away from trees.		
25	**26**	**27**	**28**	**29**	**30**	
Remove and burn wild and diseased fruit trees.				Spread limestone according to soil test. 1 ton/acre = 5 lb./100 sq.ft.		

November

After harvest I don't have as much time to amble through the orchard. There are fall chores to be done, wood to get in for winter, and other cold weather preparations. The orchard seems sadly neglected now that the fruit is in the cold cellar. When I do walk through the orchard, it's usually very early in the morning and I'm wearing orange — keeping my eyes out for deer or hunters.

Young trees are too succulent and deer are too hungry to be scared away when forage is scarce. In November I patch up the electric deer fence, making sure the wires are tight and there are no short circuits. Once I tracked a buck right up to the fence, then lost the trail, only to find where it had bounded about fifteen feet away after having touched the wire. I don't think he will try again.

This is also the time to check the mouse guards around the young trees. First, I rake away the mulch into piles between the rows. Admittedly there are plenty of mice present when one uses a mulch, and often I send them scurrying as I break up their cozy homes. My cats have learned to follow close this time of year. Then I clear away the ground around the trunks and make sure that the mesh mouse guards are slightly dug into the soil. Finally, I make sure that there is a mound of coarse gravel around each guard to further discourage rodents.

My final chore to put the orchard to bed is to paint the south side of the trunks of the young trees with a white latex paint to prevent bark splitting caused by the winter sun. After I'm done the block of new trees looks like a grove of birch saplings. I'm glad they are not birch. Other trees might need less care during the year, but I can think of nothing more satisfying than the personal commitment and relationship I have with my fruit trees.

Using Pesticides Safely

Agricultural chemicals have been used to support an unsustainable system of agriculture. This system is still regarded as necessary to feed the earth's burgeoning population. However, with new knowledge we are now able to start designing agricultural systems that will be self-regulating so that agricultural chemicals will no longer be necessary. Meanwhile, it may be necessary to use the tools of poison in an informed, safe way.

A pesticide is a poison with a relative toxicity, specific targets and dosages, and various known and unknown side effects. Toxicity is multifaceted. Fish, birds, insects and mammals are affected in infinitely varying ways by chemicals of any origin, and every member of every species is sensitive to varying degrees. New aspects of toxicity are becoming evident. The traditional lethal dose index (LD 50) is no longer sufficient since the discovery of genetic mutagens.

An example of this is Captan, a petroleum-based wettable powder fungicide with a relatively non-toxic LD 50 of 9000 mg./kg. It would take over a pound of this chemical, ingested orally, to kill a healthy 150 pound person. It is usually mixed with water at the rate of two tablespoons to a gallon, enough for several young trees, or six pounds to 300 gallons, enough to cover an acre of mature trees. Captan is an extremely effective fungicide, and has been considered very safe.

Now it is known that Captan is a mutagen capable of causing chromosomal damage, and a potential carcinogen. This puts it in a new category of toxicity about which not enough is known and for which there is no meaningful scale of risk. People who have been using Captan for years without protection have been exposing themselves to a potentially cancer causing chemical. DO NOT USE CAPTAN without a respirator and full protective gear, no matter what the label says. Exposure to all chemicals should be kept to a minimum. Learning proper spray procedures is an important personal commitment.

There are no easy answers to the endless compromises made in choosing a pesticide spray. There is rarely a "right" or "wrong" pesticide. For example, synthetic pyrethroids are relatively non-toxic to humans but broad-spectrum and deadly for beneficials whereas Imidan is highly toxic to mammals but selective to target pests, sparing many beneficials. Funginex, a powerful eradicant and systemic fungicide, is not eligible for organic programs because of its

103

synthetic nature, but lime-sulfur which is harmful to leaves and beneficials and not very effective is acceptable. It is these paradoxes that make decisions difficult.

Even the "milder" chemicals sold in hardware stores and "organic" compounds should never be used casually or carelessly. Sensitivity to chemicals varies from person to person. Study all you can about pesticide safety — your extension office has literature and will give you information about free training courses.

Treat all pesticides like the poison they are. Always wear rubber boots, waterproof clothing, a hat (or hood) which protects the neck, rubber gloves, goggles and a respirator. The outfit may not be the ultimate in comfort, but it would be foolish to try to grow nutritious fruit without putting your own health first.

The most common cause of pesticide poisoning for applicators is through the skin. Some concentrates can be absorbed through the skin in seconds. If any pesticide is spilled on your skin wash it off immediately. Careful handling and protective clothing are the keys to safe application of sprays.

Safety to the environment is equally important to personal safety. Never try to spray on windy days, and always be conscious of the spray "drift" which inevitably occurs. Fish are sensitive to pesticides, especially rotenone, so keep clear of watercourses. Never overspray. If thorough coverage is required as in the case of fungicides, spray just to the point where there is some drip off the foliage.

Consideration of neighbors is important. It is very advisable to notify neighbors of your intentions to spray, to tell them what you are spraying, and to let them know that you are using approved materials. Diplomatic pre-spray notification will go a long way toward defusing neighbors' fears. Remember that neighbors have the right not to be exposed to your chemicals, and some states are in the process of defining the concept of chemical trespass.

The Maine Organic Farmers and Gardeners Association has developed a "No Spray Register," which allows landowners to notify neighboring pesticide users that they do not want their land to be contaminated with pesticides, through drift or misapplication. This is an important first step in communication and cooperation between pesticide users and those who have the right not to be exposed to pesticides.

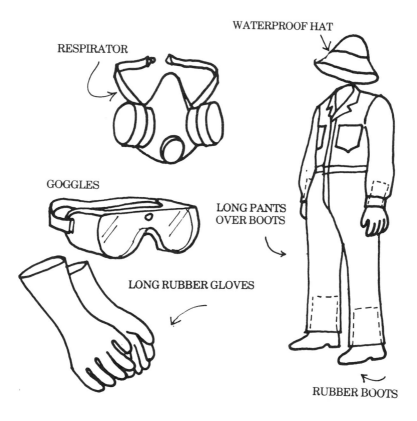

RESPIRATOR

WATERPROOF HAT

GOGGLES

LONG PANTS OVER BOOTS

LONG RUBBER GLOVES

RUBBER BOOTS

105

Bacillus Thuringiensis — A Microbial Insecticide

Bacillus thuringiensis (Bt) is a bacterium that is cultured in laboratories to produce toxic spores. This product is then blended with inert carriers, anti-evaporants and stabilizers. It is marketed as a microbial insecticide under numerous brand names such as Dipel, Bactur, Thuricide and Biotrol. It was discovered and later isolated in a laboratory culture in a dying caterpillar. Bt is an insecticide that is specific to the larvae, caterpillars and worms of the Lepidopterae family (butterflies and moths). These larvae have a biological peculiarity — an alkaline digestive tract. When Bt is ingested by these larvae the chemical action of their gut releases a protein crystal which cuts up their stomach lining. The larvae stop eating and die within a few days. No serious effect on other living species has yet been discovered.

Many orchard pests are lepidopterae larvae including: tent caterpillar, leafrollers, gypsy moth, budmoth, codling moth, leafminer, oriental fruit moth and winter moth. Any of these larvae feeding on apple leaves sprayed with Bt can ingest a toxic dose. Codling moth and leafminer do not feed on leaves for long, burrowing into fruit or leaves early in their life. If spray timing is perfect many of these pests can be controlled, especially if a feeding attractant is added to the Bt. Skim milk has been a moderately effective homemade feeding attractant. Commercial preparations such as Gustol or Nu-Lure Insect Bait are even more effective. Nu-Lure can be used with other insecticides as well.

The effective rates of Bt vary for each species. It may be economical for many orchardists to add Bt to most pre-bloom sprays and in alternate sprays after bloom. Since it breaks down in light after a few days in spite of added stabilizers it is best to spray in the evening when most caterpillars start to feed.

Bt is species specific. It is relatively safe for humans, beneficial insects and bees. Conventional growers use Bt because it is extremely effective and can be used up until the date of harvest. There is reason to suspect that lepidopterae will take a long time to develop resistance to the physical killing action of Bt, but nature is full of surprises and insects are extremely resilient.

106

Botanical Insecticides

Botanical insecticides are those poisons that are manufactured from plants. These plants develop the poisons as protection against being eaten. Botanical insecticides are generally accepted under organic management because they are bio-degradable. They are broken down into harmless components by the microbial decomposition process. Unlike their synthetic counterparts they do not accumulate in living tissue or harm soil organisms when they become breakdown products.

This does not mean that these insecticides are safe for humans, beneficial insects or other life. They can even be more toxic than synthetic pesticides although they do not have known mutagenic properties. They should be used only as a last resort when preventative ecological controls do not prevent pest damage from crossing the economic threshold. Almost any poison that kills target pests eventually affects the rest of the eco-system in a negative way.

Rotenone is probably the most used and recognized plant-derived insecticide. It can be processed from a number of tropical plants. It is commercially available in 1 percent and 5 percent concentrations and in botanical blends. Rotenone was originally developed by South American natives to kill fish. It is also toxic to birds and, in spite of some claims, mammals including humans. It is a broad spectrum insecticide meaning it will kill most insects on contact. Although many organic gardeners have employed it especially to kill potato bugs, orchardists should avoid its use because of its harmful ecological impact (technically termed high ecological profile). Only a serious plum curculio or apple maggot infestation could warrant its use.

Pyrethrum is a popular natural insecticide extracted from the pyrethrum flower, an African Chrysanthemum. It is such an effective insecticide that a synthetic formulation of its most active ingredient, d-trans alletherin, is used in numerous household insecticides such as Raid. Chlorinated pyrethrins, termed pyrethroids, which are intensively used in orchards are based on the natural molecular structure of pyrethrum.

Pyrethrum is a broad-spectrum short-lived insecticide that is relatively non-toxic to mammals. Since it has little residual activity it can be used as a "rescue" spray for most insect infestations. Care must be taken in its storage as it deteriorates rapidly. Pyrethrum extract can be

107

prepared by the orchardist if the correct variety is grown. Spray rates depend on the strength of the product formulation.

Ryania was used extensively in many orchards to control codling moth until the 1970 s. It is prepared from a large woody shrub, ryania speciosa, that grows in Trinidad and parts of Venezuela. Ryania is a selective insecticide that will kill or stun codling moth and oriental fruit moth but will not harm beneficial insects or mites. Ryania has recently been reintroduced to North American trade channels.

Triple Plus is a botanical blend of rotenone, pyrethrum and ryania that has reappeared in the market. Triple-Plus is the brand name that has replaced the old Tri-Excel label. This powerful formulation has been used for curculio and apple maggot infestations.

Nicotine extract from the tobacco plant was popular as an orchard insecticide in the 40 s and 50 s and is still available today as Black Leaf 40. It is extremely toxic and has a long residual action which precludes its use in ecological orchard management.

Other botanicals that have been used in orchards include, quassia (cassia) from a Jamaican tree, sabadilla, made from a tropical American lily, and false hellbore made from a North American flower. There has been little research or commercial use of these products but they seem to be typical of most botanicals — broad spectrum but biodegradable.

Whenever an orchardist uses botanical insecticidal sprays he/she should remember the words of Carl Huffaker the dean of California IPM entymologist , "When you kill off the natural enemies of the pests, you inherit their work."

Diatomaceous Earth

Diatomaceous earth is processed from sedimentary deposits of microscopic one-celled plants called diatoms. These shell deposits consisting of 90 percent silica can be of either fresh or salt water origin, and exhibit slightly varying properties. The silica deposits are carefully ground into glass-like, razor sharp shards. The size of the grind is important as they should not be large enough to harm warm blooded animals. Often a blend of sizes is used. Once ground they are dried and become highly absorbent. Diatomaceous earth is also used extensively as a filter material but this is a different product and should not be used for insecticidal purposes.

Diatomaceous earth kills insects by puncturing the shell or skin and/or absorbing waxy coverings and internal fluids. Either way the insect dehydrates and dies within days. This is a broad spectrum insecticide — it does not differentiate between pests and beneficials. Mammals, birds and fish are not harmed by it, bees are protected by their hair and earthworms can digest it. Like all dusts it should not be inhaled.

Some brand name formulations include Permaguard, Fossil Flower, and Bonterra. Some products may include natural pyrethrums and synergists like piperonyl butoxide (which can be derived from petroleum or peppercorns).

The best method of application is dusting. Diatomaceous earth clings best to wet surfaces but can be washed off. It can be sprayed with water (slightly abrasive to nozzles) but is only effective after it has completely dried. It may be possible to time the application to affect a pest population without damage to beneficials. Only an informed orchardist can decide whether the application of a broad spectrum insecticide is necessary.

Enzyme Ticket Pesticide Detectors

A reliable new detector for organophosphate and carbamate pesticides has been developed by Midwest Research Institute. The inexpensive device uses an enzyme to detect the presence of pesticide in a water sample. The enzyme "ticket" provides a safe/not-safe response sensitive to parts-per-million concentrations of pesticides. The test takes less than five minutes.

These pesticide detectors cost about four dollars each and may be a real asset to orchardists. Recommended uses include:

- Checking safe worker re-entry following pesticide spraying of the orchard.
- Monitoring spill cleanup and decontamination.
- Determining extent of drift during pesticide spraying.
- Check for toxicants in run-off and streams.
- Check for residues in cider.

Insecticide Rates

WP = wettable powder   EC = emulsifiable concentrate

Insecticide	Formulation	Rate	Cautions
Rotenone	1% WP	8T/gal	(4,5)
	5% WP	6T/gal	(4,5)
Ryania	50% WP	8-10T/gal	(1)
Pyrethrum	(3) WP	(3)	
Triple/Plus	WP	8-10T/gal	(4,5)
Superior oil	90 sec. EC	10T/gal	(2)
Insecticidal soap	EC	6T/gal	
Diatomaceous .earth	WP	(3)	
Bacillus thuringiensis (Bt)	WP	2-4T/gal	(2)
Malathion	25% WP	3T/gal	
	50% EC	1T/gal	
Imidan	12.5% WP	4T/gal	
	50% WP	1T/gal	

1) Use with bait such as Nu-Lure (1t./gal).
2) Incompatible with sulfur, bordeaux fungicides.
3) Depends on formulation - read the label.
4) Apply with electrostatic duster if possible.
5) Toxic to fish.

Use a respirator when mixing and applying all insecticides.
With help from Bill Wolf and Patti Nesbitt of Necessary Trading Co.

Fungicide Rates

WP = wettable powder   EC = emulsifiable concentrate

Fungicide	Eradicant hours at 50 F	Formulation	Rate	Cautions
Micro-fine sulfur	0	90% WP	2 ½T/gal	(1,2,6,7,10,11)
Flowable sulfur (THAT Big 8)	0	64% EC	(3)	(1,2,6,7,11)
Lime sulfur	12	29% EC	4-6T/gal	(1,2,4,6,10,11)
Bordeaux	0	8-8-100	2-4T/gal	(2,6,10,11)
Basic copper sulfate (fixed copper)	0	29% EC	1T/gal	(5,7,10,11)
TOP COP with sulfur	0	—	1T/gal	(1,2,5,7,10,11)
Polyram	0	80% WP	2T/gal	(9)
Captan	24	80% WP	1T/gal	(1,9,12)
Manzate	24	80% WP	1.5T/gal	(9)
Cyprex	36	65% WP	.5T/gal	(9,13)
Phygon	48	50% WP	.5T/gal	(8,9)
Funginex	72	1.6% EC	(9)	(9)

1) Incompatible with oil spray.
2) Use with surfactant or spreader-sticker.
3) See following chart.
4) Do not mix with other spray materials.
5) Toxic to fish.
6) Do not apply in hot weather.
7) Do not use during bloom.
8) Do not use after petal fall.
9) Check label instructions for various fruits and local regulations.
10) Use in cool, moist weather. Overuse will cause leaf damage.
11) Tank agitation necessary.
12) Use with extreme caution. See March, November.
13) Applicator sensitivity in some individuals.

Use respirator when mixing and applying all fungicides.

Flowable Sulfur Rates

These are the current recommendations for Stoller's "THAT Big 8": 64% sulfur

APPLE, PEAR	Scab	pre-bloom	1-2 t./gal
		post-bloom	1 t./gal
	Powdery Mildew	pre-bloom	1-2 t./gal
		post-bloom	1 t./gal
PEACH	Leaf Spot		
	Brown Rot	pre-bloom	1-2 t./gal
	Powdery Mildew	post-bloom	.5-1 t./gal
CHERRY, PLUM	Leaf Spot		
	Brown Rot	pre-bloom	1 t./gal
	Brown Spot	post-bloom	.5-1 t./gal

Synthetic Chemical Pesticides

There are dozens of synthetic pesticides used in orchards today which are not mentioned in this book because of their toxicity to applicators and beneficial organisms. The synthetic pesticides that are mentioned are few in number, chosen for their relatively low eco-profile. The fungicides were covered in the March chapter as well as "All Purpose Spray." The only two synthetic chemical insecticides mentioned are Malathion and Imidan. This does not indicate any superior characteristics of these two materials as much as it indicates the great lack of other selective, safe synthetic insecticides.

Malathion is available as a liquid or a powder. It has an oral LD50 of 1375 mg/kg in tests with rats so it should be used with caution. It is used in the suggested spray program only for the control of aphids and only when aphids are threatening young trees. Overuse will harm beneficial insects.

Imidan seems to be the synthetic insecticide least harmful to beneficial insects in the orchard. It has a LD50 of 300 mg/kg in tests with rats and must be used with extreme caution. It gives effective control of codling moth, apple maggot, redbanded leafroller, pear psylla, curculio and many other insects. Imidan is not very effective against aphids, hence the use of Malathion as above.

DECEMBER

- Varmint Protection

- Abandonment of Orchards

				1	2	3
				Burn corrugated cardboard codling moth traps		
4	**5**	**6**	**7**	**8**	**9**	**10**
Order insect traps for next year.				Check fences, mouseguards.		
11	**12**	**13**	**14**	**15**	**16**	**17**
Check and renew deer repellents.				Order nursery stock early.		
18	**19**	**20**	**21**	**22**	**23**	**24**
Give a disease resistant tree to a friend.				Cut down diseased wild trees.		
25	**26**	**27**	**28**	**29**	**30**	**31**
Burn the yule log bright.				Sample the cider barrel.		

December

113

December

There is little calling me to visit the orchard in this first month of winter except the good habit or a good snowstorm. Seldom is the year that I need the snowshoes until later in the season, but I usually get an opportunity to wax the skis and take a run through the orchard before the new year. The quiet is powerful as I glide down the rows. The steam from my body rises straight on the cold windless day as I pause at the end of the row.

The trees have hardened off well this year. There has been steadily colder weather since harvest, good soaking rains and no sudden thaws or cold snaps. The trees I set out six years ago were damaged at that time by a warm autumn followed by a sudden 40 degree drop on Christmas eve. It was too cold too fast, then a January thaw compounded the injury. Those trees have been dwarfed ever since. Many growers lost sizeable portions of their orchards that year. This year the twigs of the new trees have a healthy blush under the cold inter bark.

My orchard rambles on over the next hill and there are blocks of trees farther away that I attend to as best I can. Many of these trees I call mine are adopted or have owners who hire me to care for their trees. My reward for pruning some trees last spring was watching an eagle fly over with a fish in his talons. Close enough to smell the fish, I became aware that I had entered another realm.

I take my time to admire the trees and the sky, then in the shelter of the barn I putter and sharpen tools. The red maggot fly traps hanging from the rafters look like ornaments, so I hang a few with the wreath on the door. Satisfied with the finishing touch of the orchard year I grab some logs for the winter fire and go in.

Varmint Protection

The amount of pressure from mammalian pests varies greatly from place to place and from year to year. Wildlife populations tend to be cyclic - some years there can be terrible mouse damage and some years very little. Prevention is important in any case as the pressure is impossible to predict. The cost of prevention is insignificant compared to potential loss. It is better to start with the best system available than to be constantly maintaining and upgrading homemade remedies. Unfortunately, there is no absolutely guaranteed prevention - under starvation conditions animals will go to extraordinary lengths to get forage.

Rodent Control — Mice, voles and rabbits can quickly girdle and kill young trees and even older trees, unless careful precautions are taken to reduce their populations in the orchard and to physically prevent them from getting to the trees. Reducing populations can be achieved by mowing the orchard regularly and keeping it clean, keeping mulch from becoming compacted and moving it away from the trees in the fall, shallow cultivation around the base of the trees, and poison bait. If poisoned oats must be used take precautions to prevent poisoning of other animals.

The very best tree guards, and the only ones I can recommend, are made from hardware cloth, three eighths or one half inch wire mesh. Initially more expensive than other tree guards, they are long lived, they do not create problems with the bark, they do not harbor pests and they are extremely effective. These mesh guards need to be checked every year to assure that they are not constricting.

Spiral plastic tree guards, foil, or treated paper wraps have many drawbacks and should be used with caution. I find them unsatisfactory for many reasons: 1) they harbor insects such as codling moth; 2) they interfere with the detection of borers and may even encourage them; 3) tree trunks stay moist almost all the time, encouraging virus and diseases; 4) sometimes they do not expand as designed when the tree grows and can constrict, even girdle the bark; and 5) the plastic degrades in sunlight, making it brittle and prone to breakage. If you use plastic tree guards be sure to remove them in the spring and replace them at the end of summer.

A mound of coarse gravel or crushed stone around the wire mouse guards will help deter rodents. The mound should be six inches high and about twelve inches in radius. Mice which forage along the

115

soil/snow interface will be discouraged before they even reach the wire mesh. If the gravel is placed when the tree is planted and if it is several inches deep, it may help prevent damage to the roots by pine voles which forage underground.

Controlling these underground pine voles is much more difficult than dealing with the above-ground meadow mice. Pine voles spend almost all their lives underground in an intricate system of tunnels. They feed on the roots of trees and in some areas they cause severe damage. Often the only signs of their presence are tunnel entrances marked by piles of fresh soil. Probing with a sharp stick will reveal underground tunnels. The recommended procedure for control is to carefully excavate some of these tunnels, put in some poison bait, then cover the excavation with a board and then soil. If the tunnel is active the voles will attempt to repair it and take the bait. Baiting the entrance openings may also work. In any case these pests can be very destructive, so control has to be consistent. Do not use mulch if pine voles are a problem.

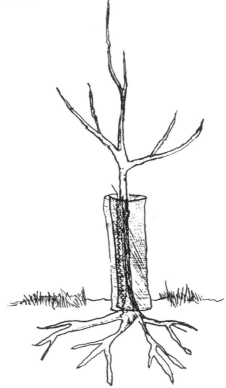

Deer Control — Electric fence is the best solution for large orchards but probably impractical for small orchards or several trees. New high-powered fence chargers and high tensile wire give effective and low cost control. Several designs have proven to deter deer.

The seven-wire outward sloping fence and the three-wire trip fence both seem to work well. Cost is well below the cost of woven wire fence of sufficient height to deter deer. Maintenance includes the need to keep weeds from shorting out the wires, but the new high voltage fences seem to be less sensitive to weeds than older types of electric fence.

The effectiveness of electric fence depends upon an initial contact and shock which quickly teaches animals not to try again. This can be done by luring the deer to the fence by looping a piece of aluminum foil smeared with peanut butter over the wire. After the initial shock, a deer will stay away from the fence even if for some reason the fence becomes deactivited.

Many people do not have enough acreage to warrant fencing, or their trees are too spread out to make fencing appropriate. To protect these trees one must use repellents which seem to be effective in inverse proportion to the hunger of the deer. Materials range from the ridiculous to the improbable, including: lion manure, bloodmeal, citronella-like "lemon rope," white reflective triangles, dirty socks and cheesecloth bags of human hair. I can attest to the latter but I don't know its duration of effectiveness. You will have to experiment to find what works best for you.

Abandonment of Orchards

Sometimes an orchardist may have to let an orchard, or a few trees, go unsprayed for a season for any number of reasons. Economic reasons, a change in the ownership, a loss of interest or time, or simply absence will mean that the trees don't get the care they should during the growing season. In this circumstance the advantages of a natural pest management program are overwhelming. The orchard that has been heavily sprayed will suffer a great deal of damage when abandoned until, after several years, it adjusts to a natural balance of insects.

Mites and aphids quickly attack the abandoned "chemical" orchard. The predators of these insects are the first to succumb to heavy doses of insecticides, and it may take years before the beneficial populations are built up enough to keep mites and aphids under control naturally.

Apple maggots will usually be present whether the orchard was heavily sprayed or not, but codling moths will definitely increase if the heavy use of pesticides has limited the number and variety of their natural predators. Sometimes a minor insect like the red-banded leafroller will flare up and ruin the fruit.

The orchard that has been managed with a minimum of pesticides will usually have good populations of beneficial insects. Natural predators will keep mites and aphids under control. Codling moths will seldom be a significant problem. Apple maggots and curculios have few natural predators and they may damage the fruit but they won't kill the trees.

Whenever the management of orchards cannot be ideally consistent the benefits of natural pest control become obvious. Working to emulate the natural balance of insects puts nature to work for you.

Appendices

- Glossary
- Bibliography
- Suppliers
- Insectiaries
- Nurseries
- Organizations
- Periodicals
- Inventory
- Metric Conversion
- Dwarfing Rootstocks
- Organic Fertilizer Materials
- Foliar Nutrients
- Spray Schedules
- Insecticide Rates
- Fungicide Rates
- Sample Scab Worksheet

Glossary

beneficial insect: insects that pollinate flowers, or that feed on or parasitize pests. They can be naturally occurring or introduced.

chemical: this term is used, somewhat incorrectly, to describe the conventional approach to agriculture. These methods are based on feeding the plant directly with soluble fertilizers and protecting it from pests and diseases with toxic sprays.

degree day: accumulated temperatures above a fixed base temperature upon which estimates of plant or insect growth are calculated.

economic threshold (treatment threshold): that size of a pest population which can be correlated with a damage level high enough to warrant treatment.

eco-profile: effects of a substance upon the entire ecosystem.

eradicant fungicide: a fungicide that kills fungi after spores have infected plant parts.

insecticide: a substance that kills or controls insects.

frass: sawdust-like excrement of insects found on fruit or on trunks usually indicating insect activity.

fungicide: a substance that kills or controls fungi

larva: the immature stage (caterpillar, maggot, grub) of moths, flies and beetles.

lethal dose index (LD50): a relative scale of toxicity based on the amount of a toxin needed per body weight to kill an organism.

organic: this term is not used in the scientific sense of a carbon-based compound. It is used to identify an agricultural approach that eschews synthetic fertilizers and pesticides while relying on ecological methods that work with nature rather than against it.

parasite: an organism that derives its sustenance from another organism, usually harming its host.

pest: an organism which is damaging to the cultivated crop.

pesticide: a substance used to control or kill pests, including insecticides, miticides, fungicides and herbicides.

pheromone: a chemical which is produced by insects for communication and/or attraction. Pheromones can be synthetically produced.

phytotoxicity: the damage caused to foliage and other plant parts by applied materials.

pomology: the science of fruit cultivation.

predator: an organism that seeks out and feeds upon another organism.

preventative fungicide: a fungicide that kills fungi by being on the plant before the fungal spore infects the plant tissue.

pupa: a stage of insect development between the larval and adult stages.

russetting: naturally occurring or chemically induced roughening of the skin of fruit. Usually yellow-brown or reddish-brown in color.

sucker: sprouts from the base of trees, sometimes interchanged with the term watersprout.

surfactant (spreader-sticker): spray material used to decrease leaf surface tension in order to allow better coverage, penetration and retention.

watersprout: vertical, non-productive, rapid growing shoots from the branches of fruit trees. Sometimes referred to as suckers.

Bibliography

Apple, J. and Smith, R. (1976) *Integrated Pest Management*. Plenum Press, N.Y. A basic text with good chapters on fruit pests.

Atkinson, D., et al. (1980) *Mineral Nutrition of Fruit Trees*. Buttersworth Publishers, Woburn, MA. The comprehensive textbook on tree feeding.

Boethel, J., et al. (1977) *Pest Management Programs for Deciduous Tree Fruits and Nuts*. Plenum Press, N.Y. Papers on I.P.M. methods in the orchard from a technical entymology conference.

Carr, A. (1979) *Color Handbook of Garden Insects*. Rodale Press, Emmaus, PA. Good color photos that include many orchard pests.

Childers, N.B. (9th edition 1983) *Fruit Science*. Horticultural Publications, Gainesville, FL. A classic college textbook. Workbook available.

Gershuny, G. and Smillie, J. (1986) *The Soul of Soil — A Guide to Ecological Soil Management*. Box 84, St. Johnsbury, VT. A comprehensive guide to soil fertility that contains all the orchardist needs to set up a fertilization program.

Hall-Beyer, B. and Richard J. (1983) *Ecological Fruit Production in the North*. RR 3, Scotstown, Quebec. Excellent guide to selecting, pruning, training and propogating of numerous varieties of cold-hardy fruit trees and shrubs.

Hill, Lewis (1977) *Fruits and Berries for the Home Garden*. Alfred A. Knopf, NY.

Koepf, H.H., Petterson, and Schaumann (1976) Bio-Dynamic Agriculture. Anthroposophic Press, Spring Valley, N.Y. This is the most practical introduction to the Bio-dynamic method available.

Logsdon, G. (1981) *Organic Orcharding — A Grove of Trees to Live In*. Rodale Press, Emmaus, PA. Useful introduction for the homestead orchardist.

Proulx, A. and Nichols, L. (1980) *Sweet and Hard Cider.* Garden Way Publishing, Charlotte, VT.

Watson, P., et al. (1975) *Practical Insect Pest Management.* Freeman and Co., San Francisco, CA. Introductory self-instruction manual.

Van Den Bosch, R. (1978) *The Pesticide Conspiracy.* Viking Press, NY. Sensational overview of "conventional" pest control practices by a pioneer I.P.M. entomologist.

Teskey, B.J.E. (1978) *Tree Fruit Production.* AVI Publishing Co., Westport, CT. Introductory text.

Suppliers

Where to get the materials mentioned in this book.

Agri-Systems International
125 W. 7th Street
Wind Gap, PA 18091
   Natur-Gro R-5O (Ryania) and Triple-Plus (Rotenone-Pyrethrins-Ryania).

Ag-Tech Instrument Co.
Box 3723 Savannah, GA 31404
   Weather instruments.

Applied Pest Management Research, Inc.
Box 938
Amherst, MA 01004
   Visual traps and adhesives.

Consep Membranes
Box 6059
Bend, OR 97708
   Pheromone traps and lures.

Down to Earth
850 W. 2nd Street
Eugene, OR 97402
   Bio-lure insect trapping systems.

Gardeners Supply Co.
133 Elm Street
Winooski, VT 05404
   Full range of orchard supplies.

Great Lakes IPM
10220 Church Road, NE
Vestaburg, MI 48891
   Monitoring products.

Green River Tools
Box 1919
Brattleboro, VT 05301
   Quality pruning tools, bird houses, etc.

Growing Crazy
2460 South Beyer Road
Saginaw, MI 48601
   Ecological orchard supplies.

Harmony Farm Supply
Box 451
Groton, CA 95444
   Complete line of ecological pest controls, fertilizers, and beneficial insects.

Micro Gene Systems, Inc.
400 Frontage Road
West Haven, CT 06516
   Codling Moth Granulosis Virus (CMGV).

Miller Chemical
Box 333
Hanover, PA 17331
   Lime-sulfur solution, Nu-Lure insect bait, and Nu-Film 17 surfactant.

M.R.I. Ventures, Inc.
425 Volker Boulevard
Kansas City, MO 64110
   Enzyme ticket pesticide detector.

Natures Way
6030 Grenville Lane
Lansing, MI 48910
  Biological and botanical pest controls.

Necessary Trading Co.
437 Main Street
Newcastle, VA 24127
  Mail or bulk order supply company with a complete line of
ecological orchard materials.

Neogen Food Tech
620 Lesher Place
Lansing, MI 48912
  Pestcaster disease and insect forecasting system.

Peaceful Valley Farm Supply
11173 Peaceful Valley Road
Nevada City, CA 95959
  Complete line of orchard supplies including beneficials.

Phenix Farm Supply
311 W. 72nd Street
Kansas City, MO 64114
  Ecological insect controls and fertilizers.

Reuter-Stokes
Edison Park
Twinsburg, OH 44087
  Predictor apple-scab and degree-day forecasting machine.

Scentry, Inc.
P.O. Box 11645 — 85061
Chandler, AZ 85224
  Formerly Albany International. Over forty pheromone lures.

Seabright Enterprises
4026 Harlan Street
Emeryville, CA 94608
  Stickum adhesive for traps.

Services Bio-Controle
2949 Chemin Ste. Foy
Ste. Foy, Quebec G1X 1P3
Pheromone traps and lures.

Stoller Chemical Co.
8582 Katy Freeway
Houston, TX 77024
or
3228 South Service Road
Burlington, Ontario L7N 3H8
"THAT" flowable sulfur, "THIS" chelated micro-nutrients and "TOP-COP" copper based fungicide.

TangleFoot Co.
314 Straight Avenue
Grand Rapids, MI 49504
Tanglefoot adhesive for traps.

Trécé, Inc.
P.O. Box 5267
Salinas, CA 93915
Pherocon (Zoecon) insect monitoring traps.

Insectiaries

Applied Bionomics
Box 2637
Sidney, BC V8L 4C1
  Beneficial predators and parasites.

Better Yield Insects
Box 3451, Tecumseh Station
Windsor, Ontario N8N 3C4
  Predatory gall midge and predator mites.

King Labs
225 Yost Avenue
Spring City, PA 19475
  Trichogramma wasps.

Metro Pest Management Consultants
Box 1029
Denver, CO 80001
  Beneficial predators and parasites.

Rincon Vitova
Box 95
Oak View, CA 93022
  Lacewings, Lady Beetles, Predatory Mites and Trichogramma Wasps.

Unique Insect Control
Box 15376
Sacramento, CA 95851
  Lady Beetles, Praying Mantis, Trichogramma wasps.

Nurseries

Boughen Nurseries
Box 12 Valley River, Manitoba R0L 2B0
   Hardy fruit trees and shrubs.

Bountiful Ridge Nurseries
Princess Anne, MD 21853

Golden Bough Tree Farm
Marlbank, Ontario K0K 2L0

Hilltop Nurseries
Box 143
Hartford, MI 49057
   Disease resistant varieties.

J.E. Miller Nurseries
Canandaigua, NY 14424

Living Tree Center
Box 797
Bolinas, CA 94924

Mellingers Nursery
2892 Range Road
North Lima, OH 44452

New York State Fruit Testing Cooperative Association
Geneva, NY 14456
   New and experimental varieties.

St. Lawrence Nurseries
RD #2
Potsdam, NY 13676
   Hardy fruit and nut trees.

Sursum Corda
RR #3
Scotstown, Quebec J0B 3B0
   Hardy fruit trees.

Vermont Fruit Tree Co.
River Road
New Haven, VT 05472
   Disease resistant varieties.

Organizations

California Certified Organic Farmers (CCOF)
Box 8136
Santa Cruz, CA 95061
Certification, information and quarterly newsletter.

Canadian Organic Growers (COG)
46 Lorindale Avenue
Toronto, Ontario M5M 3C2
Information and quarterly newsletter.

Ecological Agriculture Projects
Box 225
Macdonald College
St. Anne de Bellevue, Quebec H9X 1C0
Library and resource facility.

Maine Organic Farmers and Gardners Association (MOFGA)
Box 2176
Augusta, ME 04330
Information, certification and bi-monthly journal.

New York State Fruit Testing Co-operative Association
Geneva, NY 14456
Information, scion and rootstock exchange.

North American Fruit Explorers (NAFEX)
c/o Mary Kurle
105 055 Madison Street
Hinsdale, IL 60521
Fruit afficionados exchange scions and information and publish Pomona a quarterly newsletter.

Northeast Organic Farmers Association (NOFA)
c/o Box 335
Antrim, NH 03440
Information, certification and a quarterly newsletter. Chapters in VT, NH, CT, MA, RI and NJ.

Organic Crop Improvement Association (OCIA)
Box 226
Derby Line, VT 05830
    Certification organization with chapters in ONT., QUE., VT, NY, MA, CA, MN and FL.

Organic Foods Production Association of North America
P.O. Box 31
Belchertown, MA 01007
    Trade association organized to establish and maintain standards of excellence for the organic food industry.

Periodicals

American Fruit Grower
37841 Euclid Avenue
Willoughby, OH 44094
    A journal that serves the needs of large scale conventional orchardists and pesticide advertisers. Numerous, useful articles make it well worth the low subscription price.

Canadian Fruit Grower
222 Argyle Avenue
Delhi, Ontario N4B 2Y2
    A brief, informative, inexpensive journal.

I.P.M. Practitioner
Box 28A
Winters, CA 95694
    An excellent newsletter that is technical in nature but very readable and practical for the small-scale orchardist.

Biodynamic Tree Fruit Newsletter
c/o Alice Bennett-Groh
RFD 1 Temple Road
Wilton, N.H. 03086
    A group networking effort with articles from the readers.

INVENTORY

- Rainsuit or foul weather gear, waterproof with a hood.
- Goggles.
- Rubber gloves and boots. Leather boots absorb and hold pesticides.
- Respirator and filters, labelled for use with agricultural chemicals.
- Insect traps and tanglefoot stickum.
- Sprayer.
- Hand lens, 10x or 20x.
- Minimum/maximum thermometer.

METRIC CONVERSIONS

unit	times	factor = unit
acres	x	.4 = hectares
ounces	x	.28 = grams
pounds	x	.45 = kilograms
teaspoons	x	5 = milliliters
tablespoons	x	15 = milliliters
gallons	x	3.8 = liters
degrees Fahrenheit	x (after subtracting 32)	5/9 = degrees Celsius

°C	4.4	7.2	10	12.8	15.6	18.3	21.1
°F	40	45	50	55	60	65	70

Dwarfing Rootstocks

Representing as it does the bridge between the fruit tree and the soil, the rootstock is an important but frequently overlooked component in the eventual degree of satisfaction to be gained from planting a fruit tree. While the commercial orchardist is more inclined to study the rootstock thoroughly before ordering trees, most home gardeners give little more thought to the subject than "Is it a dwarf?" This can be a recipe for disappointment.

Soil and climate conditions vary enormously and while it is possible to find appropriate rootstocks within the considerable variety available across the continent, locally available choices are usually quite restricted. More often than not garden center personnel don't even know what roots are available, let alone anything about what conditions they prefer. "Dwarf" trees are certainly the most popular with the average gardener but "dwarf" within the nursery trade encompasses a vast range of sizes, and dwarf trees are far from problem free.

Because of their reduced vigor, dwarf trees are less able to fend for themselves than are their larger cousins. Dwarfed trees cannot as a rule tolerate competition from insects, diseases, weeds or other plants. They are usually significantly less cold hardy than larger types. Whats more, most dwarfing rootstocks have really poor roots, and unless the trees are well staked their entire (short) lives there is a good chance that they will uproot or at least tip over in a wind. Most gardeners do not have the horticultural skills required for maximum success with dwarf trees, although many can get by if the trees are planted in a sheltered area. The person planting the family orchard will be much happier with larger trees that don't need so much babying.

Not all so-called dwarfing rootstocks produce the same sized tree, and the easiest method of comparison is to express the final size of an unpruned dwarf tree as a percentage of the size the same variety would attain when grafted onto a standard rootstock. Roughly put, a standard rootstock like "Dolgo" will produce a tree some 30 metres tall. Thus a rootstock producing a tree that topped out at 15 metres could be described as making a 50 percent tree and so on. Hence the designations of "semi-dwarf" and "semi-standard" which expand on the simple dwarf/standard dichotomy.

Most of the commonly available dwarf and semi-dwarf rootstocks (up to about 40 percent trees for dwarf, and from 40 percent to 70 percent for semi-dwarf) are introductions from the East Malling

Research Station in England. The Malling stock consists of a series of roots numbered M1, M2, etc., up to M27, as well as a series designated MM101, MM102, etc., up to MM111. This latter series was introduced in the 1950 s specifically to furnish rootstock resistant to woolly apple aphids. Of these 40 or so Malling rootstocks only a handful, M7, M9, M26, MM106, and MM111 are relatively easy to find.

M7 is a general all purpose rootstock producing a 40 percent to 60 percent tree. It is not particularly well rooted or hardy, and it suckers badly. However, it will tolerate a wide range of soil conditions.

M9 produces a 25 percent to 35 percent tree with a very poor root system which is quite brittle. Regular watering is important. Trees are early to bear and the fruit ripens about a week earlier than on other stock.

M26 produces a 30 percent to 40 percent tree that while better anchored than M9 will always need support. This root is susceptible to burr knot at the graft union, which will be several degrees less winter hardy than the rest of the tree.

M27 is a recently introduced "super dwarf" producing a 15 percent tree. Its root system is nearly non-existent and it is not particularly hardy. As a root for patio trees it has potential.

MM106 produces a 45 percent to 65 percent tree that is 30 percent more productive than M7 under the same conditions. It is fairly well anchored but susceptible to collar rot and should not be planted in persistently wet soils.

MM111 is the hardiest and best anchored of the Malling rootstocks, but it is a semi-standard at 65 percent to 80 percent. Tolerant of variable soil conditions.

With the exception of MM111 none of the Malling roots is suitable for use in a region colder than Zone 4 (USDA). MM111 will probably be acceptable in much of Zone 3 (USDA).

With increasing vigor (size) comes increasing hardiness, and in colder zones a number of semi-standard and standard rootstocks make even commercial apple production possible. These come from various parts of the world and include Antonovka, Anis, Baccata, Borowinka and Beautiful Arcade. Each has particular characteristics and the northern reader is referred to more specialized texts.

The major drawback to larger trees is that they are somewhat harder to spray and to pick, however judicious pruning can hold the height to relatively modest levels, and the overall ease of care may suggest that they have a place in the family orchard. **Bart Hall-Beyer**

Dwarfing Rootstocks and Tree Size

SPECIES Rootstock	Size of Tree or degree of dwarfing	Bearing Age	Yield (approx)	Spacing	Number per acre
APPLE					
M27	15%	2-4 yrs.	< 1 bu.	3' x 12'	1000
M9	25% - 35%	2-4 yrs.	1 bu.	6' x 12'	605
M26	30% - 40%	2-4 yrs.	1 bu.	10' x 14'	240
M7	40% - 60%	3-5 yrs.	3-5 bu.	14' x 20'	180
MM106	45% - 65%	3-5 yrs.	4-6 bu.	15' x 22'	140
MM111	65% - 85%	3-5 yrs.	5-7 bu.	16' x 24'	115
Seedling	100%	3-9 yrs.	6-10 bu.	24' x 32'	55
PEAR					
Quince	50%	2-4 yrs.	< 1 bu.	6' x 12'	605
Seedling	100%	3-7 yrs.	2-5 bu.	18' x 26'	95
SWEET CHERRY		3-4 yrs.	2-3 bu.	20' x 28'	75
SOUR CHERRY		3-5 yrs.	2-3 bu.	16' x 24'	115
PEACH		3-5 yrs.	2-5 bu.	16' x 24'	115
PLUM		3-5 yrs.	1-3 bu.	16' x 24'	115

(Adapted from The Spraysaver Apple Calendar (1979) by S. Page)

134

Organic Fertilizer Materials

Mineral Nutrient	Soil Application	Foliar Spray
Nitrogen	Compost, green manures, Chilean nitrate (16-0-0) Fish meal	Fish emulsion
Phosphorous	Colloidal phosphate (0-20-0) Bonemeal (0-26-0)	
Potassium	Sul-po-mag or K-Mag (0-0-22) 11% Mg	
Calcium	Calcitic or dolomitic limestone or agricultural gypsum	Calcium chloride Chelated calcium
Magnesium	Sul-po-mag (K-Mag) Dolomitic limestone	Epsom salts Chelated Magnesium
Boron	Borax* or Borate*	Solubor
Sulfur	Flowers of sulfur Potassium sulfate Gypsum	Flowable sulfur
Zinc, Manganese, Copper, Iron	Sulfate form	Chelates
Other trace minerals	Compost Fritted trace elements	Liquid seaweed extracts

* Concentrated boron is toxic. Avoid overuse or uneven spreading.

While most of these materials mentioned are generally recognized as organic it is the responsibility of certification organizations to make this decision. Check all materials with a certification organization if you will market organic fruit. Potassium sulfate, Solubor, certain chelates, fritted trace elements, and fish emulsion may be regulated while others like foliar urea, potassium nitrate, and superphosphate may be allowed.

Detail on the analysis, availability and use of these materials can be found in The Soul of Soil - A Guide to Ecological Soil Management.

Foliar Nutrients

Element	Source
Copper	Basic copper sulfate or Bordeaux spray see Fungicide Table
Boron	Solubor 20% 1T/gal
Zinc	Zinc chelate 1T/gal or Polyram as fungicide
Magnesium	Magnesium sulfate 15T/gal or Magnesium chelate 1T/gal
Calcium	Calcium chelate 2T/gal or Calcium chloride 3T/gal do not mix with solubor
Nitrogen	Urea (low biuret urea) 3T/gal at petal fall for apples only or fish emulsion 3T/gal

Delayed Dormant Spray

Bud Stages: Silver Tip, Green Tip, Half-inch Green

Insect Pest	Organic Control	Chemical Control
Mites Aphids Scales Psylla	superior oil — split sprays one half at green tip, one-half at tight cluster or full dose at one-half inch green	none needed

Disease	Organic Control	
Scab	sulfur, except not within 30 days of oil. Bordeaux	Pre-infection: Polyram Post-infection: see eradicant table (March)
Powdery mildew Brown rot (cherries)	sulfur, except as above cultivate, remove all mummified fruit	

Fertilizers		
All trees	apply compost early foliar feed at one-half inch green for known deficiencies	

See November for pesticide rates.

Pre-Bloom Spray

Bud Stages: Tight Cluster, Pink, Bloom

Note: control insects only when traps indicate thresholds are crossed.

Insect Pest	Organic Control	Chemical Control
Tent caterpillar	Remove manually, or spot-spray Bt	Spot-spray Imidan before bloom
Tarnished plant bug European apple sawfly	Observe traps weekly, record weekly catches	None needed yet
Leafminers, winter moth	Bacillus thuringiensis	No insecticides In Bloom!!!
Eye-spotted bud moth	Observe traps	
Aphids	No control needed at this time.	

Disease		
Scab	*Sulfur Bordeaux table (March)	Pre-infection: Polyram Post-infection: see eradicant
Fire blight	Prune, disinfect tools bloom	"TOP COP" (Stoller) with sulfur at 10%
Powdery mildew	*Sulfur	
Brown rot (cherries)	Cultivate, remove all mummified fruit; sulfur	
Black knot	*Sulfur	Polyram or Phygon

* Do not use sulfur within thirty days of oil

Fertilizers		
All trees	Apply compost early Foliar feed at early pink	

See November for pesticide rates.

Post-Bloom Spray

Note: control insects only when traps indicate thresholds are crossed.

Petal Fall (75% Flowers Gone)

Insect Pest	Organic Control	Chemical Control
(Note: control only when monitoring shows evidence)		
Plum curculio	Triple-plus	Imidan
Codling moth	Bt with bait	Imidan according to
Ryania with bait		to trap data
	Trichogramma release	
Leafroller	**Bt**	Not necessary
Plant bug	**Triple-Plus**	In severe cases use
		Imidan

Disease
(Note: observe weather to time scab sprays accordingly)

Scab	Sulfur	Pre-infection:
	Bordeaux	Polyram
		Post-infection:
		see eradicant
		table (March)
Powdery mildew	Sulfur	
Brown rot (cherries)	Cultivate, remove all mummified fruit; sulfur	
Black knot	Sulfur	Polyram or Phygon
Fire blight	Prune, disinfect tools	Streptomycin — consult extension agent "TQP COP" with sulfur

Fertilizers

All trees	No more compost
	Foliar feed all trees at petal
	fall especially boron and magnesium
	according to leaf analysis.

See November for pesticide rates.

First Cover Spray

Ten Days After Petal Fall

Insect Pest   **Organic Control**   **Chemical Control**
(Note: control only when monitoring shows evidence)

Insect Pest	Organic Control	Chemical Control
Plum curculio	Repeat Triple-plus	Imidan
Codling moth	Bt with bait or ryania with bait*	Imidan according to trap data
Leafroller	**Bt**	Not necessary
Mites, aphids Gypsy moth	Observe buildups Bt with bait	Imidan
Japanese beetle	Milky spore disease	

Disease
(Note: observe weather to time scab sprays accordingly)

Disease	Organic	Chemical
Scab	Sulfur Bordeaux primary spore discharge ending soon	Pre-infection: Polyram Post-infection: see eradicant table (March)
Powdery mildew	Sulfur	
Brown rot (cherries)	Cultivate, remove all mummified fruit; sulfur	
Black knot	Sulfur	Polyram or Phygon
Fire blight	Prune, disinfect tools	Streptomycin — consult extension agent

Fertilizers

All trees	Final foliar feeding spray

* Insect bait is a feeding attractant. See November for pesticide rates.

Summary Sprays

Note: control insects only when traps indicate thresholds are crossed.

Insect Pest	Organic Control	Chemical Control
(Note: control only when monitoring shows evidence)		
Apple maggot	Red ball traps Rotenone Bordeaux spray	Imidan
Codling moth	Bt with bait or ryania with bait*	Imidan according to trap data
Red-banded leaf roller	**Bt**	Imidan according to trap data
Aphids	Control ants Insecticidal soap	Spot application — Malathion
Borers	Insecticidal soap on trunks, probe with wire	Rotenone/diatomaceous earth paste on trunks
Pear psylla	Dust with limestone or diatomaceous earth	Imidan if severe

Disease

Scab	When primary discharge is over, protectant sprays are seldom necessary	
Black rot, bitter rot	Sanitation, Bordeaux	Polyram
Sooty blotch, fly speck	These diseases cause minor cosmetic damage, rarely need control	
Brown rot	Sanitation, cultivation Sulfur, especially pre- harvest on peaches	Polyram

* Insect bait is a feeding attractant. See November.

See November for pesticide rates.

Insecticide Rates

WP = wettable powder   EC = emulsifiable concentrate

Insecticide	Formulation	Rate	Cautions
Rotenone	1% WP	8T/gal	(4,5)
	5% WP	6T/gal	(4,5)
Ryania	50% WP	8-10T/gal	(1)
Pyrethrum	(3) WP	(3)	
Triple/Plus	WP	8-10T/gal	(4,5)
Superior oil	90 sec. EC	10T/gal	(2)
Insecticidal soap	EC	6T/gal	
Diatomaceous earth	WP	(3)	
Bacillus thuringiensis (Bt)	WP	2-4T/gal	(2)
Malathion	25% WP	3T/gal	
	50% EC	1T/gal	
Imidan	12.5% WP	4T/gal	
	50% WP	1T/gal	

1) Use with bait such as Nu-Lure (1t./gal).
2) Incompatible with sulfur, bordeaux fungicides.
3) Depends on formulation - read the label.
4) Apply with electrostatic duster if possible.
5) Toxic to fish.

Use a respirator when mixing and applying all insecticides.

142

Fungicide Rates

Fungicide	Eradicant hours at 50 F	Formulation	Rate	Cautions
WP = wettable powder			EC = emulsifiable concentrate	
Micro-fine sulfur	0	90% WP	2 ½T/gal	(1,2,6,7,10,11)
Flowable sulfur (THAT Big 8)	0	64% EC	(3)	(1,2,6,7,11)
Lime sulfur	12	29% EC	4-6T/gal	(1,2,4,6,10,11)
Bordeaux	0	8-8-100	2-4T/gal	(2,6,10,11)
Basic copper sulfate (fixed copper)	0	29% EC	1T/gal	(5,7,10,11)
TOP COP with sulfur	0	—	1T/gal	(1,2,5,7,10,11)
Polyram	0	80% WP	2T/gal	(9)
Captan	24	80% WP	1T/gal	(1,9,12)
Manzate	24	80% WP	1.5T/gal	(9)
Cyprex	36	65% WP	.5T/gal	(9,13)
Phygon	48	50% WP	.5T/gal	(8,9)
Funginex	72	1.6% EC	(9)	(9)

1) Incompatible with oil spray.
2) Use with surfactant or spreader-sticker.
3) See following chart.
4) Do not mix with other spray materials.
5) Toxic to fish.
6) Do not apply in hot weather.
7) Do not use during bloom.
8) Do not use after petal fall.
9) Check label instructions for various fruits and local regulations.
10) Use in cool, moist weather. Overuse will cause leaf damage.
11) Tank agitation necessary.
12) Use with extreme caution. See March, November.
13) Applicator sensitivity in some individuals.

Use respirator when mixing and applying all fungicides.

Flowable Sulfur Rates

These are the current recommendations for Stoller's "THAT Big 8": 64% sulfur

APPLE, PEAR	Scab	pre-bloom	1-2 t./gal
		post-bloom	1 t./gal
	Powdery Mildew	pre-bloom	1-2 t./gal
		post-bloom	1 t./gal
PEACH	Leaf Spot		
	Brown Rot	pre-bloom	1-2 t./gal
	Powdery Mildew	post-bloom	.5-1 t./gal
CHERRY, PLUM	Leaf Spot		
	Brown Rot	pre-bloom	1 t./gal
	Brown Spot	post-bloom	.5-1 t./gal

Sample Scab Worksheet:

Date	Time leaves wet	Temp.	Time leaves dry	Temp.	Elapsed wetness time	Av. temp.	Bud stage	Infection Yes/No	Treatment
4/28	7:15 PM	54	6:00 AM	47	10:45	50.5	½" green	No	
4/29	4:00 AM	48	10:00 AM	49	6:00	48.5	½" green	No	
5/3	10:00 AM	52	5/4 6:00 AM	51	20:00	51.5	tgt clstr	Yes	lime-sulphur 7AM 5/4
5/5	12 noon	56	7:00 PM	54	7:00	55	tgt clstr	No	
5/10	6:00 AM	54	5/12 8:00 PM	46	62:00	50	tgt clstr	Yes- heavy	Manzate 2PM 5/10
5/16	4:00 PM	60	5/17 6:00 AM	55	14:00	57.5	Pink	Yes- light	Sulphur 7PM 5/16
5/24	7:30 AM	58	4:30 PM	54	8:00	56	Bloom	No	
5/28	10:00 PM	49	5/29 2:30 PM	52	14:30	50.5	Bloom	Yes	Polyram 7AM 5/29
6/5	4:30 PM	56	6:30 PM	55	2:00	55.5	Petal fall	No	
6/10	2:00 AM	59	8:30 AM	63	6:30	61		No	
6/16	9:30 PM	61	6/17 6:00 AM	65	8:30	63		Pos- sible	Manzate 7AM 6/17

End primary scab season

In this example scab infection worksheet the orchardist has a permanent record of weather and scab infections. In most commercial orchards, up to 12 fungicide sprays would have been applied in the same amount of time. By keeping such records, the attentive orchardist can minimize the use of fungicides.